CONNECT

Junior High ®

What Does It Mean to Be a Catholic?

Catechist's Guide Author: Rev. Alexander M. Santora

Silver Burdett Ginn

Morristown, NJ

MW01103256

Program Consultant   Robert J. McCarty

Program Advisors   Josephine Actis   Anthony Bellizzi   Kathleen Holtsnider
William J. Freburger   Maureen Ouellette

Catechist's Guide Contributors   Rev. David A. Costa   Dr. James Kenny
Mary Jane Kenny   Joseph Moore

The Publisher would like to give special thanks to Greg Dues, Tom Everson, and Claire Manes, who made significant contributions to the development of the *CONNECT Junior High* program.

Nihil Obstat   Reverend Anselm Murray, O.S.B., *Censor Librorum*

Imprimatur   †Most Reverend Frank J. Rodimer, Bishop of Paterson
June 23, 1993 (Youth Magazine); August 13, 1993 (Catechist's Guide)

The *nihil obstat* and *imprimatur* are official declarations that a book or pamphlet is free of doctrinal and moral error. No implication is contained therein that those who have granted the *nihil obstat* and *imprimatur* agree with the contents, opinions, or statements expressed.

Acknowledgments

Scripture selections taken from *The New American Bible with Revised New Testament*, Copyright ©1986 by the Confraternity of Christian Doctrine, Washington DC, are used by license of the copyright owner. All rights reserved. No part of *The New American Bible with Revised New Testament* may be used or reproduced in any form, without permission in writing from the copyright owner.

A Vision of Youth Ministry, ©1976, and *Sharing the Light of Faith: National Catechetical Directory for Catholics of the United States*, ©1979 by the United States Catholic Conference, Department of Education, Washington, DC. All rights reserved.

The Challenge of Adolescent Catechesis: Maturing in Faith, ©1986 by the National Federation for Catholic Youth Ministry, Washington, DC. All rights reserved.

Credits and acknowledgments continue on the inside back cover, which constitutes an extension of this copyright page.

CONTENTS

A Culmination . . . For many students, junior high school marks the closing of eight years of more formal religious education.

CONNECT Junior High builds upon the strong foundation developed in Silver Burdett Ginn's THIS IS OUR FAITH, Grades 1–6, and provides an excellent alternative to a textbook approach to religious education.

CONNECT
Junior High
The ideal transition to an interactive model of catechesis for today's younger adolescents.

SUGGESTED GRADE LEVEL ORGANIZATION

GRADE 7	GRADE 8
Who Am I?	The Challenge of Relationships
Who Is Jesus?	Our Church Yesterday and Today
What Does the New Testament Say?	The Question of Morality
What Does It Mean to Be a Catholic?	Responding to Social Issues

GRADE 7 or 8

What About Sexuality?

Meeting the Needs of Junior High

CONNECT Junior High

And a Beginning . . . *For many students, junior high school can mark a new dimension in their life as Catholics: the beginning of a youth ministry program!*

Each of the nine themes in **CONNECT Junior High** has a separate full-color YOUTH MAGAZINE, which uses a six-session format. In addition, every theme has its own easy-to-use, full-color CATECHIST'S GUIDE.

CONNECT Junior High emphasizes the **experience** of our faith while relating its essential **doctrinal content.**

After Breaking the Ice, each session follows an effective three-step process:

1. Starting Out
2. Exploring
3. Connecting

The Journey Continues!

For the faith-life of **high school** youth in parish programs—*CONNECT: A Program for Adolescent Catechesis.*

Adolescents Today and Tomorrow!

CONNECT Junior High

A Time for Change

The junior high years have been called the "quicksilver years" to describe the nature of seventh and eighth graders. These young people are setting out on what is one of the most intensive periods of growth in all of human life: puberty. As a result of the changes associated with puberty and early adolescence, the youth are themselves very changeable—one day (even one minute!) children; the next, young adults; and back again.

This age group has often presented difficulties for parish religious education programs. Junior high youth may find textbooks dull and boring and become unresponsive to the catechetical models that worked well in the past. They seem to need catechesis that is more interactive and community-based than didactic, that expresses our Catholic faith message in terms of their life issues rather than as materials to be learned.

Youth ministry models of catechesis, already popular among high school adolescents, seem to be an appropriate response for this age group. At the same time, though, junior high youth are not high schoolers. The issues they face and their perspectives on life are maturing, but still need to be defined in terms of the junior high experience. These young people want to participate in lively discussions and activities rather than listen to lectures, but the discussions and activities have to be more concrete than theoretical in order to accommodate the early adolescent's stage of intellectual development.

What is needed, what catechists of junior high youth have always asked for, is a way to make the transition from a textbook model of catechesis to a model of adolescent catechesis within the setting of total youth ministry. In response, we have published *CONNECT Junior High*. This program has as its primary audience catechists, youth ministers, and junior high youth involved in parish programs of religious education. Through *CONNECT Junior High*, we hope to address the needs expressed by you, the person who relates to young people week by week and month by month. In addition to seeking your opinions, we questioned directors of national youth organizations as well as junior high adolescents, who themselves previewed the design and content of the YOUTH MAGAZINES.

Catechesis and Youth

CONNECT Junior High can be situated within the context of a parish's religious education program for junior high youth. In the United States, two important Church documents have been published on the nature of youth ministry and adolescent catechesis within the parish. These are *The Challenge of Adolescent Catechesis: Maturing in Faith* and *A Vision of Youth Ministry.*

The document *Maturing in Faith* situates the Christian catechesis of young people in "a comprehensive, multifaceted approach to ministry with youth" (Fifth Foundational Principle). *Maturing in Faith* suggests fourteen faith themes that may serve as a framework for catechetical programs with younger and older adolescents. By presenting these faith themes, catechists and youth ministers may pass on the Catholic faith tradition to young people in a coherent manner that respects the participants' development.

As with all Christian catechesis, catechesis of youth stems from one source—God's divine word revealed in Jesus Christ—and studies this source in its many manifestations, or signs. The principal signs of catechesis are biblical, liturgical, ecclesial, and natural. (From *Sharing the Light of Faith: National Catechetical Directory for Catholics of the United States,* #41–46.)

Models for Adolescent Catechesis

Parishes establish and run catechetical programs in a variety of ways. For those parishes changing from a textbook model to a more comprehensive youth ministry program, a **small-group** approach may work best. This is the most common type of program for adolescent catechesis and the one for which *CONNECT Junior High* is ideally suited. Meeting once a week (or every other week) for 60 to 90 minutes, catechists and youth ministers facilitate the catechesis of adolescents in small groups of about 8–12 participants. Faith themes are often treated in a minicourse format of varying length.

Two other models, which have been in use with high school teens, may also be adopted for junior high programs. In a **retreat/catechetical day** model, young people gather together at regular times throughout the year for an extended period (a day or weekend, for example) to participate in catechesis, sharing, prayer, and worship. In a **large-group** model, sometimes called the "youth group model," the adolescents come together in large groups. After icebreaking activities, a catechist or youth minister may give a presentation on a certain topic, after which the group might divide into smaller groups for more informal faith sharing.

Total Youth Ministry

The term *total youth ministry* refers to a parish's overall ministry to young people aged 12 and up, which necessarily includes, but also extends beyond, adolescent catechesis. The document *A Vision of Youth Ministry* proposes two goals for youth ministry.

1. Youth ministry works to foster the total personal and spiritual growth of each young person.
2. Youth ministry seeks to draw young people to responsible participation in the life, mission and work of the faith community.

A Vision of Youth Ministry, p. 7

To achieve these goals, seven components are considered integral to a total youth ministry program. For those parishes introducing junior high youth to an already-existing program, or starting up any type of youth ministry program, the realization of these goals may well be a gradual process. Effective catechesis for adolescents does not require a full-blown, total youth ministry program, although the latter will certainly enhance the former and vice versa.

Word   Ministry of the word involves the evangelization and catechesis of youth, helping them to hear, understand, experience, and proclaim the good news of Jesus Christ.

Worship   This ministry involves young people in the many and varied worship experiences of the Church, including the Eucharist and other sacraments, nonsacramental liturgies and prayer services, and individual prayer.

Creating Community   Relationships are extremely important to young people, and fostering community among junior high adolescents is an essential function of youth ministry. A communal sense may flourish through catechesis, worship, social activities, and service programs.

Guidance and Healing   These ministries are necessary if youth are to work through the suffering and hurts that may hinder their development. Ministers of guidance and healing need not be limited to priests, catechists, or youth ministers. In peer ministry programs, young people can be ministers of guidance and healing to one another.

Justice and Service   After washing the disciples' feet at the Last Supper, Jesus said: "I have given you a model to follow, so that as I have done for you, you should also do" (John 13:15). Engaging younger adolescents in justice and service embodies this mission of Jesus.

Enablement   Through a ministry of enablement, young people and adults alike are empowered to be ministers of the gospel message, leading others to God as they themselves are being led.

Advocacy   In their roles as catechists and youth ministers, adults can represent and support the needs of youth in parish and local communities as well as in the community at large. This encouragement by concerned adults serves to strengthen an adolescent's self-esteem.

The *CONNECT Junior High* Program

CONNECT Junior High currently includes nine themes, or minicourses, for junior high catechesis. Each theme consists of six 60-minute sessions. For each theme, you may purchase a CATECHIST'S GUIDE for yourself and a YOUTH MAGAZINE for each group member.

The *CONNECT Junior High* themes were written for, and are optimally suited to, a small-group model of catechesis. It is expected that this approach will foster community-building in a catechetical setting. However, if your parish is looking to adopt other models of catechesis, the YOUTH MAGAZINES may also be used as the catechetical portion of a retreat/lock-in or as the basis of a monthly catechetical day. Likewise, parishes using a large-group format may choose to distribute the MAGAZINES as part of the activities or to supplement the program.

Other Essential Components

In addition to the catechetical themes, *CONNECT Junior High* offers a PROGRAM DIRECTOR'S MANUAL (PDM), a valuable resource that contains further information about catechesis and youth ministry. It includes planning materials for retreats, parent-youth meetings, and prayer celebrations for use by large or small groups. The PDM also has a separately bound GUIDE FOR COMMUNITY SERVICE. This GUIDE presents the catechetical background for Christian service and suggests a number of service projects for use by groups or individuals.

As part of your parish's order, you will also receive a blackline master supplement entitled *CONNECT with Music*. This correlates contemporary and religious music to the nine themes of *CONNECT Junior High* as well as to the fourteen themes in the high school *CONNECT* program. The supplement may be reproduced for reference by individual catechists and youth ministers.

CONNECT Junior High Themes

Since *CONNECT Junior High* themes are purchased separately, their use and sequence are variable and are best decided according to the requirements of a particular parish. The content of the themes is based upon the guidelines outlined for younger adolescents in *Maturing in Faith.* However, to suit the needs of you, the people we serve, we have adapted the themes presented in that document as well as added themes not explicitly listed.

Four of the *CONNECT Junior High* themes are suggested for use in seventh grade and four are suggested for use in eighth grade. (Four six-week courses constitute a full 24-week year of catechesis.) The ninth theme, *What About Sexuality?*, may be used as an elective in either grade.

These grade distinctions reflect the common practice in junior high catechetical programs, but it is important to stress that the grade distinctions are only suggested by us. You alone are the best judge of the backgrounds, interests, and abilities of your junior high adolescents and may find that themes suggested for eighth graders are appropriate for seventh graders.

Within each grade, the order in which you present the themes may also vary. Our listing reflects a topical progression from life experience issues (personal growth and relationships) to key teachings of our faith (Jesus, Scripture, and Church) to themes that discuss ways we live out our faith (Catholic traditions, morality, and issues of justice).

Further Reading

Benson, P., et al. *The Quicksilver Years.* San Francisco: HarperCollins, 1987.

The Challenge of Adolescent Catechesis: Maturing in Faith. Washington, DC: National Federation for Catholic Youth Ministry, 1986.

Goodwin, Carole D. *Quicksilvers: Ministering with Junior High Youth.* West Mystic, CT: Twenty-Third Publications, 1992.

Rice, Wayne, et al. *Creative Resources for Youth Ministry* (6 vol.). Winona, MN: St. Mary's Press, 1981-1982.

Strommen, Merton. *Five Cries of Youth* (2nd ed.). San Francisco: HarperCollins, 1988.

A Vision of Youth Ministry. Washington, DC: United States Catholic Conference/Department of Education, 1976.

Suggested Grade-Level Organization

Grade 7	Grade 8
Who Am I?	The Challenge of Relationships
Who Is Jesus?	Our Church Yesterday and Today
What Does the New Testament Say?	The Question of Morality
What Does It Mean to Be a Catholic?	Responding to Social Issues

Grade 7 or 8
What About Sexuality?

Part 2

EARLY ADOLESCENCE

The Drama of Change

"What's the matter with that kid?" is a common question from observers of twelve- and thirteen-year-olds. How did that sweet, happy little tomboy suddenly turn into a sullen, critical, moussed and eye-shadowed young woman? Why does that freckle-faced, easygoing ballplayer now spend most of his time in his room, talk in monosyllables, and otherwise avoid contact with his family?

The young person between the ages of twelve and fourteen years old is in the first stages of adolescence. Even casual observers note that adolescent change can be sudden, dramatic, and all-pervasive as a child begins to develop physically, intellectually, and emotionally. Other changes, which are less easily observed but nonetheless significant, include changes in moral judgment and spiritual outlook.

Developmental Theory

Physical growth proceeds in an orderly fashion during childhood. The infant moves from crawling to standing to walking in a systematic, predictable way. Developmental theorists tell us that growth in other areas, such as intellectual ability, emotional expression, moral judgment, and spiritual outlook, also progresses in predictable stages. Moreover, just as physical growth is enhanced with proper nurturing, so also is advancement in other areas stimulated by challenges appropriate to the given stage of development. But while physical growth is often orderly and rather inevitable, emotional, moral, and spiritual growth may be stunted, diverted, or enhanced by influences in the growing child's environment.

Understanding the stages of development is important for the catechist working with younger adolescents. People can grasp concepts, values, and judgments only in relation to their developmental level. We may often get a sense of ideas one level above our present level; indeed, such challenges may make us reach and grow. But concepts too far beyond our range have little meaning for us. Catechists need to be aware of the developmental levels of their group members in order to be more effective communicators.

A temptation of developmental theories, though, is that we may forget a very important principle. Because every

person is unique and individual, people grow at their own pace, proceeding through stages of development in their own unique and individual ways. Passage through the stages usually follows the same sequence but not at the same time or in the exact same way for each person.

Also, we may try to make value judgments about the various stages, thinking, for instance, that "Higher is better" or "Let's move our young people to a higher stage." But just as an eight-month-old who learns to crawl is doing exactly what an eight-month-old is meant to do, the child who is at a child's stage of moral development or the adolescent who is at an adolescent's stage of spiritual development is exactly where he or she is supposed to be. Our goal is not to move children to adolescent reasoning or to make adolescents think like adults. Rather, it is to accommodate the various developmental stages of our group members and respect the value of each stage.

Upon first learning about developmental theory, some may also be eager to cast everyone into a particular stage, but this is neither helpful nor wise. Although we operate at one particular developmental level most of the time, we can operate at a lower stage under certain

physical development in antisocial or destructive ways: drinking, smoking, drugs, sexual activity, shoplifting, vandalism, or fighting. These behaviors are often attempts to impress peers by "proving" that one is grown up.

Implications for Catechists

1. Provide constructive ways to boost younger teens' self-esteem in an accepting environment, where participants don't have to prove themselves. Ensure that, though perhaps no one is good at everything, every group member has an opportunity to succeed at something.

2. Avoid making the young people feel ashamed or guilty about their interest (or lack of interest) in sexual matters: it's part of normal adolescent development. Young teens like to show off for members of the opposite gender, often by "playing dumb" or making smart remarks. Emphasize the importance of respecting themselves and others. Do not tolerate sexual harassment or put-downs, and teach the young people not to tolerate them, either.

3. Emphasize non-competitive games and activities that don't require much strength or skill. Avoid forcing anyone to participate in an activity that makes him or her feel embarrassed or awkward. Don't allow making fun of or drawing attention to any group member's appearance or state of physical development.

4. Be patient. Behaviors that would be considered immature in adults are normal at this age. Expect group members to be silly, restless, moody, loud, clumsy, and unpredictable. They can also be loyal, enthusiastic, energetic, idealistic, and open. Let them know that you like and accept them.

circumstances. Also, people can imitate actions of a higher level that they see modeled about them. Instead of trying to categorize individuals, it's more beneficial to use information about development to effectively communicate with young adolescents.

Growing Physically

Though there is no American "rite of passage" for young people that crosses all cultural boundaries, there is the universal passage—puberty—through which all boys and girls must proceed.

Puberty, which denotes the physical changes that accompany adolescence, marks the beginning of the transition from childhood to adulthood. Physical changes usually begin between the ages of ten and fourteen. They generally occur earlier in girls, although each individual proceeds through puberty at his or her own pace. As a result, there may well be a large range of maturity levels (in appearance and behavior) among your group members.

At this age, young people gain a new awareness of their bodies: their own and others'. They are often self-conscious about their appearance and dissatisfied with their development, wondering if they are "normal" and worrying that they are too tall, too short, too fat, too ugly—just plain "too . . . " Young adolescents begin to be curious about sexuality and become concerned about the impression they're making on members of the opposite gender. Some adolescents express this anxiety about their

Growing Intellectually

It's no accident that tasks such as designing and carrying out scientific experiments or comparing different forms of government or different economic systems are not usually found in elementary school curricula but are progressively introduced in junior high, high school, and college. Developmental theory states that, beginning around the age of twelve, children begin to develop the capacity for formal reasoning. Only with formal reasoning can we approach "what if" problems, holding different ideas in mind simultaneously and organizing them in a systematic way.

Such a capacity opens a new intellectual world to the junior high adolescent. The young person still learns much through concrete experience but is beginning to be capable of logical reasoning. However, the new ability does not appear overnight. The young person moves gradually from learning based on concrete experience to learning through formal reasoning. Not all group members will be equally comfortable with abstract reasoning, and while he or she may be a student of history, the junior high adolescent is very much attracted by lessons centered in the present.

Implications for Catechists

1. Use stories based on real-life examples and experiences to introduce ideas. Refer to current events, TV shows, and popular music.

2. Pose problems and questions relating to the present. Theoretical or philosophical problems may bore this age group easily.

3. Encourage the group members to pray and express religious ideas in their own words, rather than simply relying on memorized prayers and definitions.

4. Expect discussions to focus on the personal experiences of the young people; at the same time, you may lead them to discuss issues with greater complexity and depth than is possible with younger children.

Growing Emotionally

The adolescent is faced with the task of answering the question "Who am I?" This simple question may lead to intense concern with the self as well as volatile mood swings. Closely related to the question of identity is the question "How do I become independent while maintaining ties to my family, friends, school, community, and Church?" The task of balancing dependence and independence can lead to outbursts against parents, defiance of rules, teasing and put-downs of younger brothers and sisters, rejection of former activities such as music lessons or Scouts, reluctance to attend family events, objection to attending Mass or Church-related activities, and frequent testing and challenging—all of which can leave adults angry, baffled, and emotionally drained.

Despite this bleak picture, the adolescent behaviors that trouble parents, teachers, and other adults are normal aspects of life. Frequently, the young teen, frightened by the challenge of becoming an independent adult, uses rebellious behavior to compensate for the fears and insecurity that life presents. Adults may not like some adolescent behavior, and they need not tolerate wrong behavior. But adults can realize that problem behaviors often represent part of the young person's efforts to mature.

Implications for Catechists

1. Recognize that self-centeredness is part of the junior high adolescent's task of finding his or her identity, but do not tolerate rudeness or disrespect toward adults or other young people.

2. Begin topics with a focus on self; then try to draw group members outside of themselves toward broader concerns.

3. Don't allow situations where any group member may feel self-conscious, put down, made fun of, or embarrassed. Accept the

young teens as they are and help them grow to become their better selves.

4. Allow the group members some freedom of choice and self-determination in making decisions and sharing responsibility for the group's activities, but do not relinquish all control.

Growing Morally

Morality involves our understanding of what is right and wrong. Here, too, the young adolescent will take a major developmental step. He or she recognizes that the peer group has standards, and the opinion of peers becomes increasingly important, with the judgments of friends beginning to outweigh those of the family.

In an effort to develop his or her own identity, the young adolescent may appear to reject societal norms—particularly those of parents, school, and Church—in favor of the peer group's. Even those adolescents who appear to be critical of their peers, rejecting conventional teen dress, taste, and values, are actually responding to the power of the peer group.

Recognizing the importance of peers is an important step in moral development. In fact, many people for the rest of their lives draw their rules and value judgments from the values of their own adult peer groups. The catechist at the junior high level will be challenged constantly by the importance of the peer group in the lives of his or her group members. Rather than attempt to supplant the peer group, build on its power.

Note, also, that junior high adolescents at this stage of moral development are personalists. Not only can they put themselves in the place of another, but they can also see themselves as others see them. New capacities for empathy and compassion are now possible, as is personal sharing at deeper levels than before.

Implications for Catechists

1. Capitalize on the importance of the peer group in the lives of the group members instead of viewing peer pressure as a problem to be eliminated or an obstacle to be overcome. Invite examples of how the young people and their friends form opinions, make decisions, and solve problems.

2. Work with the junior high adolescent's natural capacity for empathy by involving the group members in age-appropriate service projects that have visible and attainable results. Encourage them to put themselves in the place of others by asking, "How would you feel if you were in that situation?"

3. Groups can exclude as well as include. Deal with any group tendency to exclude certain people. Encourage the participants to form compatible subgroups rather than assigning them to particular groups, but don't let the same people stay together all

the time. Mix the groups to encourage everyone to get to know one another.

4. Look to the peer group to find examples of virtue in your students. For example, young teens are often very supportive of their friends, sharing possessions, talking on the phone, and spending time together. Don't always point out the shortcomings of adolescent culture. Look for and praise positive qualities demonstrated by teens and their TV, movie, music, or sports heroes.

Growing in Faith

Junior high adolescents look to groups to validate their faith experience. Their religious beliefs, values, and practices are defined in relationship to those of a group. In childhood, the influential community is usually the family. As a child enters adolescence, however, allegiance begins to shift from the family to the peer group. The young teen's growing desire for independence often results in a rejection of all forms of authority, including Church leaders and their teachings. An increased capacity for intellectual reasoning may lead adolescents to question or doubt previously held religious beliefs and practices. At this age the young person may begin to dislike or openly refuse to attend Mass. The faith handed down in childhood may no longer be adequate.

On a more positive note, the importance of relationships during adolescence can enhance the spiritual development of the group members. They are growing in their ability and desire to maintain a personal relationship with God. They are able to take on more responsibility for their religious practices. Sharing their beliefs (as well as their doubts) with others their age can affirm and strengthen their faith and help make it truly their own.

Implications for Catechists

1. Liturgies and prayer services can enhance the group experience, especially when the group members help plan and carry out these services. Retreats (one-day or overnight) can foster community as well as build faith. It also helps if every session can include group prayer of some variety.

2. Allow the young teens to express their religious questions and doubts as the first step in exploring the answers. Help them persevere through their doubts rather than always trying to answer (or even deny) their questions.

3. Avoid putting young teens into situations in which they feel they must choose between being a good Christian and fitting in with their friends and peers. Remind them that God loves and accepts them as they are and understands that we're all imperfect.

4. Provide projects and activities that give group members opportunities to use their talents and idealism to put their faith into practice. Involve the young teens in planning and organizing activities.

The Ambivalent Self

The junior high adolescent may be as confused as his or her parents are by the new person he or she is becoming. Trying simultaneously to establish a new role within the family, develop satisfactory relationships with peers, and cope with a rapidly changing body, the young person is often full of inconsistencies. Psychologists tell us that change is the most difficult experience with which people must cope. If so, early adolescence must be one of the most difficult periods of life.

The junior high adolescent is faced with many challenges. For the young person who suffers from self-criticism and self-doubt, the catechist can emphasize his or her worth as a person loved by God. For the young person who feels isolated and friendless, the catechist can strive to develop community and compassion within the group. For the young person who is focused solely on self, the catechist can gently introduce concern for others. For the young person feeling antagonistic toward all authority, the catechist can creatively present the example of Jesus, who emphasizes not rules but caring for our neighbors.

As young people with a newly awakened sense of self and a growing realization of the importance of relationships with others, junior high adolescents are ready for new and deeper insights into the good news of Jesus.

Part 3

PLANNING THE SESSIONS

An Alternative Approach

A small-group model of catechesis distinguishes *CONNECT Junior High* from textbook-based religious education programs for seventh and eighth graders. The small group approach considers the faith development of the whole person by sharing ideas and feelings, recounting experiences, and communicating faith beliefs from one generation to the next.

> In the life of a community, young people and a few significant adults learn to listen to one another, and in doing so, to hear God speak. As they try to help each other express in words the truths they experience, they learn a living theology. In this kind of community youth have a mutual ministry to each other. They share themselves, their convictions, their faith with each other.
>
> *A Vision of Youth Ministry*, p. 16

For junior high catechesis in parish programs, a small-group model may be preferable because young people at this age have a strong need to feel a sense of belonging to a group that shares interests, beliefs, and goals. In the small group, junior high adolescents can find a comfortable environment to speak out freely and share what they really feel or think, to explore the doubts or questions that often arise at this age, and to experience affirmation and community with peers and adults.

The Catechist and the Small Group

A distinctive element of the small-group model is the role of the catechist, who may be characterized in three ways:

- more as a participant than as an instructor;
- more as a facilitator than as an authority figure;
- more as the creator of an atmosphere of trust and openness than as a judge of the participants' knowledge or opinions.

Instruction, authority, and knowledge are still important in the small group, although they are not as prominent as in a textbook model. Catechesis in this approach is a group activity. Though led by an adult, the group members learn from the discussion, comments, questions, and shared experiences of others: young people and catechist.

Any adult working with junior high adolescents faces a difficult task, one demanding a delicate balance of openness and control. Young people at this age are a mix of child and young adult. They aren't ready for total freedom, thus the structure and direction of the session need to be controlled by the catechist or anarchy may result. On the other hand, early adolescents are too old to accept passively explanations or exercises they consider "babyish." Challenge the group, since they will certainly challenge you! Allow the group members to participate in some decisions about the sessions and to bear some of the responsibility. Work with them patiently to help build their skills of planning, organizing, and leading.

This type of relationship requires trust among all the participants. Each person in the group must demonstrate respect for the opinions and beliefs of others. As catechists, we should be willing to share our own responses to discussion questions (while avoiding preachiness), and take seriously the responses of the group members. Don't be afraid to admit that you don't have all the answers. Be willing to meet the kids at their level, not always relating to them "from above" or expecting them to think or act like adults.

An image that might effectively describe the small-group model is *pilgrimage*. As believers in Jesus Christ, we are on a pilgrimage, or journey, to God. As adult believers, we may be further along or more experienced than the young people, but we are involved in the same journey and experience similar struggles, questions, and doubts. However, each person's journey is his or her own, to work out in a unique way. We can help and guide our group members on their journeys, but we can't make the journey for them or eliminate the struggles they face. You may often find that your participation in these sessions helps you along your own journey.

Leading Small Groups

The following suggestions may help you facilitate your small group and create a community atmosphere. You may wish to review this list with the group members since everyone should be expected to observe the principles of respect, confidentiality, and freedom.

Sit close together. Be sure that you and the group members are able to face and make eye contact with one another. To reinforce the notion that it's not a classroom session, if there is a way to avoid rows of desks, use it, even if it seems unusual;

library tables, floor pillows, or even a stairwell could provide a more suitable small-group environment.

Respect one another. Allow no putting down, mocking, or excluding members of the group. Remind the young people to put Christian beliefs into practice by treating one another as they'd like to be treated.

Encourage openness and honesty. Allow group members the freedom to <u>not</u> share their answers, which will help ensure that the answers they do share are honest. More importantly, try to create an atmosphere that will make the young people feel comfortable enough to want to share.

Listen attentively to one another. Don't tolerate interruptions, distractions, or rudeness. The group could formulate a set of behavioral guidelines that each person would promise to follow. Remind group members of these rules, but try to treat them as young adults by not scolding them.

Keep the discussion open and accept all opinions. Avoid putting down the young people or rejecting their ideas, and don't allow them to treat one another disrespectfully, either. This doesn't mean that you shouldn't state your own opinions or remind the group of Church teachings, but your role is one of guiding and helping rather than judging and criticizing. Show empathy and support their self-esteem.

Invite each person to share stories from his or her own experiences. Junior high adolescents learn a great deal from discussions of concrete examples. But don't allow anyone (including yourself) to dominate the conversation. Remind everyone of the importance of confidentiality: the things people share should always remain within the group.

Seek help when necessary. At times you may encounter young people who are in situations (perhaps involving addiction, abuse, or suicide) that require professional help. *CONNECT Junior High* is not a therapy session. Do not try to solve problems that you may not be qualified to handle. You might feel the need to contact a parent or professional; talk it over with your program director or pastor first.

Don't act shocked or disapproving about anything the young people say. Sometimes group members are just trying to get a reaction from you. Encourage them to share their feelings honestly, concentrating on the message behind their words. Remember that feelings are neither right nor wrong—only behavior can be judged as moral or immoral.

Allow time for silence. Don't get nervous if you ask a question and no one responds right away; give the group members some time to think. (If it's possible that they didn't understand the question, rephrase it.) You might want to start them off by giving your own response once in a while, but don't dominate the discussion and don't act as if your answer is the only possible one.

Encourage the participants to respond to and support one another. Build an environment in which everyone is affirmed and accepted for who they are, each person's contributions are valued, and a small faith community can develop. Maintain the sessions as a place where each young person feels accepted for who he or she is and challenged to become a better person.

Be yourself. Don't try to become someone you're not: you don't have be or act like a young person to relate to the group members. Allow them to get to know you, but don't pretend to be one of them. As a role model, your behavior and interactions with the group members may teach them more about being a Christian than whatever they might remember of the content of a session. Who you are is more important than what you say.

Use meaningful music. Playing instrumental music to help set a meditative mood is only one way to utilize music during prayer. Popular, contemporary songs may (and should) also be used. (Ask volunteers to bring in songs that relate to the coming week's topic.) Encourage everyone to participate by singing as well as listening.

Use a variety of prayer styles. Reflective passages, Scripture readings, and traditional prayers are commonly used prayer styles. You may also wish to explore other styles, such as gesture, song, dance, and art. Gently introduce the group to new and meaningful prayer experiences, but be careful not to overwhelm them. Young people at this age may be ready for brief and simple guided meditations, but lengthy periods of silent prayer, when overdone, can lead to giggles instead.

Pray aloud spontaneously. Spontaneous prayer, in the participants' own words, is a good method with small groups. With younger adolescents, it may be helpful to ask them to write down a brief prayer first, then share it aloud. (As with discussions, no one should feel obligated to participate in vocal prayer.) Try not to rely on rote, memorized prayers too often.

Include a closing ritual. Close the prayer time by inviting the group members to join hands and sing a song, offer one another a sign of peace, or pray together a familiar prayer such as the Lord's Prayer or an original prayer created by members of the group.

Junior High Adolescents and Prayer

A number of opportunities for prayer exist within the *CONNECT Junior High* sessions. Each session closes with a brief time of prayer, but you may also wish to begin the session with a prayer (ideally, after Breaking the Ice) or pause at an appropriate point during the session. These opportunities can build prayer skills that the group members may use on their own during the week. The following suggestions are meant to help make the experience more meaningful.

Involve group members in planning. Including the group in planning and preparation can help make their prayer more meaningful. Ask in advance for participants to suggest and bring in readings or music. Eventually, with training and practice, the young people can take on more responsibility for leading the prayer time.

Foster a sense of closeness. Invite everyone to sit close together in a circle, perhaps on pillows, blankets, or throw rugs. Sitting physically close reinforces the idea that *CONNECT Junior High* goes beyond a textbook model and helps foster a sense of spiritual and emotional closeness.

Create a prayerful atmosphere. Dim the lights and perhaps light a candle in the center of the circle to focus the group's attention. Any meaningful object can serve as this type of concrete focal point. The object may be religious (such as a crucifix, Bible, or icon), but it doesn't have to be. Flowers or a poster can do just as well. Allow group members to bring in symbols that are significant to them.

CONNECT Junior High Sessions

Each *CONNECT Junior High* theme, or minicourse, is divided into six sessions of 60 minutes each. Time frames are suggested for all of the activities, but they need not be strictly followed. For instance, ten minutes might be suggested for a given discussion, but you might not want to cut people off at that point if the discussion is going well.

The reaction of the group may also affect a session's structure. Some groups are less able to keep a discussion going; in that case, you could make further use of the audiovisuals, alternatives, and optional activities suggested in the CATECHIST'S GUIDE. You might also find that your group benefits from a short stretch break (perhaps including snacks). Try not to omit the time devoted to prayer; dropping this element could give the group the impression that prayer isn't very important.

Breaking the Ice

Breaking the Ice is a group activity meant to foster community as the young people are first arriving and settling in. Its primary purpose is to break down barriers between participants and create group unity by involving everyone in a shared, cooperative activity. For junior high adolescents, an icebreaker is also an effective way to expend some physical energy while having fun.

Assume that everyone—including yourself—will be involved in the icebreakers. Your own enthusiasm and participation can be the best model. (Peer pressure may persuade any reluctant young people.) However, don't force anyone who really objects to participating; find him or her a different role, such as scorekeeper. Don't permit onlookers to make fun of the participants or make them feel self-conscious.

Breaking the Ice is suggested as the starting point of every CONNECT Junior High session. Although its topic is related to the ideas discussed later, it is not essential for the group's understanding of the session. The main function of Breaking the Ice is to enhance a community perspective which is integral to the small-group model as well as to the CONNECT Junior High Process described below.

The First Session The first time the group comes together for a theme, it might be good to add an icebreaker in which participants introduce themselves. This is especially necessary if groups are reorganized after every theme.

Other Uses for Icebreakers While Breaking the Ice is designed to begin the session, you may also use icebreakers to break up sessions. This can be helpful, for example, if you do two sessions back-to-back in a two-hour format (such as a day of reflection). Even during a single 60-minute session, a fun, active break can rejuvenate the group or burn off some excess energy. Finally, never hesitate to create or use an icebreaker of your own or an appropriate one suggested by the group members.

The CONNECT Junior High Process

The CONNECT Junior High Process is a practical method that you can use to organize a session. The Process occurs over three stages: Starting Out, Exploring, and Connecting. These stages focus on interacting relationships—those among the young people and those between the young people and the catechist. (You are as much a participant in the Process as they.) This Process is not teacher-centered, but group-centered. Through the group's interaction, there is an opportunity for faith learning, sharing, and growing for everyone.

1. **Starting Out** Having gathered as a group in Breaking the Ice, the young people take a little time to enter into the actual session. This stage allows for a gradual entry into the topic and helps establish an effective environment for catechesis and sharing. The content of this stage may not be overtly religious; the purpose of Starting Out is simply to introduce the lesson as it pertains to the lives of the group members. The techniques for this stage vary and may include reading a section in the YOUTH MAGAZINE, participating in an activity, or responding to questions.

2. **Exploring** The Exploring stage incorporates the faith message of the session and is usually the core of the session's catechesis. Several methods may be used for this purpose. For example, Exploring may expand upon one or more of the points in Starting Out, or it may invite the group members to deeper reflection and discussion of the faith message.

3. **Connecting** This last stage makes the connection between our personal/communal lives and our faith. It's an integration step, attempting to bring the faith we profess into our own life experience. Group members look (by means of questions, activities, or discussion) at concrete ways of expressing and applying their faith. This stage also involves a prayer, short prayer service, or blessing, in which the group members affirm that our faith is our own personal gift from God, but it is lived out best in communion with others.

Additional Features of CONNECT Junior High

The Optional Activity This activity appears only in the CATECHIST'S GUIDE and is meant to be used if you wish to extend the session's 60-minute length. It is suggested at the point in the session to which it is best suited. The Optional Activity may also be helpful if a particular discussion or activity just isn't working or begins to lag.

Alternatives Whereas the Optional Activity is an additional activity, Alternatives are sometimes listed in the CATECHIST'S GUIDE to provide another method (frequently using a different learning style) for doing an activity that is already described as part of the session.

Annotations In certain instances within the CATECHIST'S GUIDE, the YOUTH MAGAZINE page is annotated. The annotations provide answers for objective questions, phonetic pronunciation keys for difficult words, explanatory notes, and so on.

Get Connected! This unique activity page (located on the inside back cover of the YOUTH MAGAZINE) is designed purely for the enjoyment of the group members. It relates to the topic of the theme, but is not meant to be taught or included as part of the session. (Being assigned to complete the Get Connected! page could diminish the group members' enjoyment of this feature.)

Other Essential Resources

Scripture Since it is the core record of our Christian faith, the Bible should have a prominent position in your meeting place. Although Scripture adaptations are printed in the YOUTH MAGAZINES, you may want to have participants read directly from the Bible. Junior high adolescents are often not skilled at reading Scripture aloud to a group. Therefore, you might want to read to them yourself, or work with group members to practice the readings. For these reasons, at least one Bible per group is essential, although one per person is preferable.

The Scripture adaptations printed in the YOUTH MAGAZINES are based on *The New American Bible with Revised New Testament*. It was chosen because it is approved by the National Conference of Catholic Bishops/United States Catholic Conference and is used in the Lectionary. We have chosen to adapt the language in order to help make the Scripture stories more accessible to junior high adolescents; adaptations also eliminate some of the more obvious sexist language.

Audiovisuals In the Theme Overview of every CATECHIST'S GUIDE, audiovisual suggestions are given for each session of the theme. Don't try to use audiovisual materials in each session. It may be better to select one or two for an entire theme. You could use them during a "break" night devoted to media (after the third session, for example). Another method is to conduct a longer session one time, starting out as a large group with an icebreaker and a media presentation, then breaking into smaller groups for the session itself.

It is important to preview any material you intend to use so that you can decide whether it will be useful and meaningful for your group. It may also be helpful to ask your program director, youth minister, or diocesan personnel to make suggestions based on what they know has worked well with other groups of young people and what is available locally.

Projects Page 26 of every CATECHIST'S GUIDE includes a list of suggested projects related to the theme. These activities are for use in addition to the six sessions. They represent a way of putting into practice the faith content of the sessions, helping the group members apply in an active, concrete way the religious concepts they've reflected on and discussed during the meetings. These projects incorporate aspects of the seven components of youth ministry and can serve as the foundation of a well-rounded parish junior high youth ministry program.

Physical Environment The surroundings of your group's meeting place can affect participation. It helps, therefore, to create a warm, personal atmosphere where you meet. This may require creativity, especially if your group meets in a classroom. Pillows, blankets, or throw rugs in a corner of the room can replace desks and chairs. Posters and wall hangings, as well as flowers and plants, add life to the meeting space.

The Holy Spirit This most essential of all resources—without which our ministry is futile—may be overlooked in all the hustle and bustle of organization and shouts of excited junior high adolescents. Before the young people arrive for each session, take a few moments to ask God for help, guidance, and inspiration, remembering Jesus' assurance, ". . . do not worry about how you are to speak or what you are to say. You will be given at that moment what you are to say. For it will not be you who speak, but the Spirit of your Father speaking through you" (Matthew 10:19–20).

WHAT DOES IT MEAN TO BE A CATHOLIC?

The question "What does it mean to be a Catholic?" can be fully answered only by first exploring the broader question, "What does it mean to be a Christian?" Roman Catholics are part of the larger Christian community, with Protestant and Orthodox Christians, and they share a number of beliefs with other Christian groups.

The *CONNECT Junior High* theme *What Does It Mean to Be a Catholic?* takes a look at many of the beliefs and practices that are especially associated with the Roman Catholic Church. These sessions attempt to reinforce the idea that, while there is a communal answer to the question posed in the theme title, every baptized Catholic must answer the question for himself or herself: "What does it mean for <u>me</u> to be a Catholic?"

The members of your group probably will vary in their previous religious training, both in the religious education classes they may have attended and in their exposure to religion at home. There may also be a diversity of cultural religious practices among them. For some, this material may be a new look, at a more mature level, at what they've already learned in elementary religious education programs. Others may be learning about the Catholic faith for the first time. Whatever the backgrounds of the participants, these sessions extend an invitation for each young person to come to a more adult appreciation of his or her faith, to begin the lifelong response to the question "What does it mean for <u>me</u> to be a Catholic?"

Early adolescence is an age of questioning, perhaps even rebellion. But many people who work with youth would say that it's often necessary for young people to turn away from what others have told them to do and believe, in order to discover what they themselves believe in. At this age, young people are very aware of and sensitive to hypocrisy; they will readily agree that Catholics ought to "practice what they preach." However, agreeing with this statement doesn't necessarily mean that they'll find it easy or always live up to it themselves—especially when this might mean being "different" from the crowd. (The same could be said of many adult Catholics.) It may be helpful to remind your group that the Church is made up of imperfect people like themselves, struggling—with the help of the Holy Spirit—to live as Jesus taught us.

As catechists, our job is not to feed our group members preprogrammed answers; that's a sure way to turn kids off. Instead, we need to enhance their critical thinking abilities, encouraging them to ask questions and helping them to find answers. We can guide them in finding ways to fit their faith into the dimensions of their own unique life experiences, as they will be challenged to do throughout their lives as adult Catholics.

Further Reading

Cruz, Joan Carroll. *Secular Saints*. Rockford, IL: Tan Books Publishers, Inc., 1989.

Dues, Greg. *Catholic Customs and Traditions: A Popular Guide*. Mystic, CT: Twenty-Third Publications, 1989.

Greeley, Andrew. *The Catholic Myth: The Behavior and Beliefs of American Catholics*. New York: Macmillan, 1991.

McBrien, Richard P. *Catholicism: Study Edition*. San Francisco: HarperSanFrancisco, 1984.

Perkins, Pheme. *What We Believe: A Biblical Catechism of the Apostles' Creed*. Mahwah, NJ: Paulist Press, 1986.

Rohr, Richard, and Joseph Martos. *Why Be Catholic?* Cincinnati: St. Anthony Messenger Press, 1989.

Session 1: A Face in the Crowd

Summary

What is a community? What kinds of communities do you belong to? What are the responsibilities and benefits of being a member of a community? These are some of the questions the young people focus on in this session. Most importantly, they will examine how God calls each of us not only as individuals, but as members of a community of faith.

The young people will respond to a questionnaire about their membership in their families, the first group they belong to. Their responses to a group inventory expand their concept of what a community is. They will recognize how Jesus lived and worshipped in a community of faith and how they are part of that community today within their own parish. By filling in a parish scorecard, the participants will determine how much of a family their parish community is and how they can make it more of a family.

Audiovisual Resources

Right Here, Right Now. (Videocassette or 16MM film)
The story of a man who accepts all types of people and teaches others to do the same.
(30 minutes, TeleKETICS, 800–989–3600)

We Are Responsible for One Another. (Videocassette)
We are called as Christians to help meet the needs of all people.
(30 minutes, TeleKETICS, 800–989–3600)

What's Right with the Church? (Videocassette)
Focus on the ongoing spirit of the Church and its place in our lives.
(30 minutes, Tabor, 800–527–4747)

Music suggestions for this session may be found in the *CONNECT with Music* supplement provided with the program.

Session 2: Characteristically Catholic

Summary

In the second session each young person is invited to recognize his or her identity as a member of the community of Catholic Christians. The young people will focus on some Catholic beliefs and practices such as the sacraments; the role of the pope; the saints; and Mary, the mother of Jesus.

Filling out a Data Card focuses group members' attention on their Baptism, which made them members of the Catholic community. The young people then name the seven sacraments. They learn about the pope's place in the Church hierarchy and are asked to find out who their diocesan and parish leaders are.

They are involved in a discussion of sainthood. Mary's role as mother of the Church is explained. Vocations are also included. The session ends with a group prayer asking God to help the Church remain one, holy, universal, and apostolic.

Audiovisual Resources

Catholic and Proud. (Videocassette)
Provides teens with a deeper understanding of their faith.
(28 minutes, Don Bosco, 800–342–5850)

Persons, Places, and Practices in the Catholic Church. (Videocassette)
Acquaints viewers with the variety of persons, places, and practices in the Church.
(20 minutes, Easton, 800–321–1724)

Understanding the Mass. (Videocassette)
An enactment of the Mass with a spirited explanation.
(55 minutes, Paulist Press, 201–825–7300)

Music suggestions for this session may be found in the *CONNECT with Music* supplement provided with the program.

Session 3: Let's Celebrate!

Summary

The seven sacraments are the Catholic community's principal ways of celebrating our journey through life. Through the sacraments of initiation, healing, and commitment, and the rituals associated with them, Catholics celebrate their personal and communal relationship with God.

This session heightens the participants' awareness of the sacraments by asking the young people to name the various "milestones," or important turning points, which may take place in a young person's life. The group members then explore the meaning and rituals of the sacraments of initiation: Baptism, Confirmation, and Eucharist. An explanation of the sacraments of healing, Reconciliation and Anointing of the Sick, follows. Finally, the sacraments of commitment, Matrimony and Holy Orders, are described. The session closes with each participant writing a prayer, asking God to help him or her be a sign—a sacrament—of Jesus' presence in his or her everyday life.

Audiovisual Resources

A Sacrament People. (Videocassette)
Focuses on each of the seven sacraments, their signs and symbols, meaning and significance.
(2 hours, 27 minutes, Brown/ROA Media, 800–922–7692)

Confirmation: It's Your Choice. (Videocassette)
The story of Jennifer and her preparation for the special celebration of the sacrament of Confirmation.
(20 minutes, Liguori Publications, 800–325–9521)

Signs and Sacraments. (Videocassette)
A penetrating look at the sacraments of initiation, healing, and commitment and the role they play in the faith community.
(2 hours, 21 minutes, Brown/ROA Media, 800–922–7692)

Music suggestions for this session may be found in the *CONNECT with Music* supplement provided with the program.

Session 4: Giving Thanks

Summary

This session explains the significance of the Mass as central to our lives as Catholic Christians. It explores the two parts of the eucharistic celebration. The Liturgy of the Word is compared to a sharing of our family stories, which help keep familiar persons and events alive. As we celebrate Jesus' presence in the Liturgy of the Eucharist, we become one with Jesus and with the Christian community.

Group members will read and consider the story of one family's Easter tradition and how thankfulness for the bounty they have is part of that tradition. A comparison is made between the Mass and a traditional family gathering. Group members are asked to write their own petitions to add to the Prayer of the Faithful. The symbolism of the bread and wine that are used for the eucharistic meal is explained. The session concludes with participants discussing ways to make the Mass more meaningful for young people.

Audiovisual Resources

Eucharist. (Videocassette or 16MM film)
Illustrates faith as a belief in the presence of Christ not only in the liturgy but in every aspect of human life.
(9 minutes, TeleKETICS, 800–989–3600)

Images of Grace: Eucharist. (Videocassette)
Unfolds the meaning of the Eucharist as a meal that transforms the community into the living body of Christ.
(15 minutes, Paulist Press, 201–825–7300)

The Mass Through a Teen's Eyes. (Videocassette)
A discussion of what to do when young people find Mass boring.
(28 minutes, Don Bosco, 800–342–5850)

Music suggestions for this session may be found in the *CONNECT with Music* supplement provided with the program.

Session 5: Prayer, Presence, Devotion

Summary

Many young people find it difficult to see God's presence in their everyday lives, as do people of every age. In this session, the young people are shown how to sustain their relationship with God. They are invited to make their personal and communal response to God in prayer and devotion. They take a contemporary look at some traditional Roman Catholic prayers and devotions.

Responses to a checklist encourage participants to look closely at ways to maintain a personal friendship with God. Participants focus on talking to God through a variety of prayer styles including Bible study, retreats, and Liturgy of the Hours. Participants enhance this discussion by adding their own knowledge of the various holy days and seasons. The Catholic use of sacramentals is described as a way to remind us of God's presence in our lives. To conclude the session, the young people invent their own "wordgrams" of Catholic terms.

Audiovisual Resources

African Saints. (Videocassette)
Acquaints viewers with several African saints.
(Four videocassettes, 29 minutes each, Don Bosco, 800–342–5850)

Holiest Week. (Videocassette)
Explains and explores the liturgies of Holy Week.
(28 minutes, Don Bosco, 800–342–5850)

Mary, Mother of Jesus. (Videostrip)
Presents Mary as a dynamic model for our times.
(60 minutes, Franciscan Communications, 800–989–600)

Prayer. (Videocassette)
"To Pray is to Live" and "To Pray is to Share" are two of the different perspectives at the heart of this program.
(42 minutes, Brown/ROA Media, 800–922–7692)

Music suggestions for this session may be found in the *CONNECT with Music* supplement provided with the program.

Session 6: Out of the Pews

Summary

In this session, the young people find out how they, as Catholics, are called to actually live their faith. Group members review the corporal and spiritual works of mercy. A checklist activity invites participants to acknowledge the works of mercy they may have tried and encourages them to practice additional ones. Looking at and discussing which works of mercy their parish and local community participate in can move the young people from an ideal to reality.

A discussion of worldwide problems and concerns (such as hunger) encourages the young people to broaden their perspective. Participants are invited to "Make a Difference!" by learning about and assisting Catholic service agencies and organizations. Group members will then write their own list of ways to help others. The session ends with an excerpt from a speech by Bishop J. Terry Steib of Memphis.

Audiovisual Resources

Everyone, Everywhere. (Videocassette or 16MM film)
A beautiful portrayal of the life of Mother Teresa.
(11 minutes, Franciscan Communications, 800–989–3600)

Lay Volunteers in Ministry. (Videocassette)
A brief description of the work of several lay organizations and their practical witness to the Gospel.
(29 minutes, TeleKETICS, 800–989–3600)

Voices for Development. (Videocassette)
A global view of development that examines the strong link between faith and social justice.
(20 minutes, Catholic Relief Services, 410–625–2220)

Music suggestions for this session may be found in the *CONNECT with Music* supplement provided with the program.

FOCUS

The moment our lives begin, we become part of the human family.

A FACE IN THE CROWD

Objectives

To help the participants:
- understand how one's family can shape a person;
- discuss the benefits and responsibilities of belonging to any group;
- discover how the parish community is called to be a family.

Materials Needed

old magazines (for Breaking the Ice) • Bible • pens/pencils • chart paper/marker or chalkboard/chalk • videocassette and VCR (for Optional Activity)

Session Outline

Breaking the Ice (10 minutes)
- Find out about some famous persons' lives.

1. Starting Out (15 minutes)
- Learn about each other's first names in "What's in a Name?"
- Explore the variety of "Family Ties."

2. Exploring (20 minutes)
- Complete a "Group Inventory."
- Read "A Common Cause" and list benefits of belonging to a group.
- Take a look at a "Personality Profile."
- Discuss the personal and communal aspects of religion in "Me, Myself, and God."
- Review the origins of the Catholic Christian community in "Jesus' Faith."
- Optional Activity: You may extend the session by adding the optional activity.

3. Connecting (15 minutes)
- Share group members' experiences of "Our Parish Family."
- Complete a "Parish Scorecard" and suggest ways the parish can improve.
- Design an ideal parish.
- Read Acts 2:42–47 and pray for the entire Church.

Breaking the Ice

Bring in some old magazines that contain profiles of various people.(Suggested titles: *Life, People, Us, Sports Illustrated, TV Guide*, or any teen magazines.) Invite each young person to select one magazine. Allow five minutes for the group members to comb through the pages and select one person they like. Either from what they already know about that person or what they read in the magazine, ask each group member to answer the following questions, then share his or her findings with the group.

- What kind of upbringing did this person have?

- How does his or her life involve working with a group of people?

Background for Session 1

The Importance of Belonging

Community is a word that young people may not use often. Yet it's a powerful influence that shapes all of us from our earliest days. In some form or another, we are always in a group with identifiable characteristics. In fact, life seems to shuffle us from one group to another: from immediate family, to school, teams, cliques, clubs, and so on.

It helps young teens to reflect on the groups they identify with and discern the benefits and responsibilities of belonging. Of course, no family or group is perfect and that fact needs to be acknowledged as well. But mining their communal experiences helps young people appreciate a key mission of Jesus: to build a living community.

Jesus believed that the community of faith must grow as people come to realize a central purpose of the human family: to be there for one another. The most common Christian prayer—the Lord's Prayer—focuses on our dual direction in life: toward God and toward one another. Likewise, the Great Commandment similarly calls us to love God and neighbor.

Community Experiences

Key elements of community experience are acceptance, respect, and affirmation. Knowing that we belong somewhere is an important psychological support. Belonging carries respect and the recognition that comes with involvement. A group affirms its members by allowing each to develop his or her unique abilities and thereby to strengthen the group. The group also asks individual members to look out for each other and support the group in return.

Often, young people, while rebelling noisily against organization, still hunger for recognition, and may create their own kinds of informal groups. It's interesting to observe in these groups the same kinds of requirements that young people might criticize in institutional groups.

Parish Community

Robert N. Bellah, author *(Habits of the Heart)* and sociologist at the University of California, Berkeley, said, "When students tell me they don't know if they believe in God, I tell them to go to church and find God reflected there in the faith and experience of the community." For all the changes in the Church in recent times, and the ongoing critiques of parish life, the most basic experience of communal Christianity still occurs in the parish setting.

Parishes differ as much as do the members and the leadership, and because of this, people may or may not be attracted by a particular parish. There are few ideal parishes; almost all need improvement. Probably most young people have at least peripheral contact with the parish community. It's helpful to discuss their parish experiences and use these as a springboard to consider how Christianity thrives in a community setting, as well as to discern how parishes as communities benefit from the contributions of their members.

Jesus didn't found a church, per se. The Church as an institution was founded by his followers as a way to live out the Kingdom of God, which is greater than any human institution. Helping young people see themselves as part of the Church as an ever-reforming community changing with time and reflecting the people who belong to it is an important goal of this session.

Reflections

1. What are some group experiences that have shaped me and how have they shaped me?
2. Do I feel community where I work and worship now? Why or why not?
3. What parish experience have I found most rewarding? How can I help my group become more involved in the parish?

1 A Face in the Crowd

What's in a Name?

Michael, Heather, Angelo, Yvette. Alone, a first name means very little. But attach it to a person and you identify a very particular someone in place and time.

Mention Cher, Madonna, or Michelangelo and you immediately think of a look, a style, or a talent. These first names say a lot. Each of us has a first name, a birth date, a personality, and all of the personal qualities that make us unique individuals.

Answer these questions about your first name.

● **How and why did you get your first name?**

_____

● **Do you have a nickname? How did you get it? Do you like it?**

_____

● **If you could pick a new first name, what would it be, and why?**

_____

1 **Starting Out** (15 minutes)
This session has a built-in introduction, which will enable each member of the group to learn about the others. First, ask everyone to read quietly and complete "What's in a Name?" on page 1 of the YOUTH MAGAZINE. Solicit volunteers to talk about their answers.

Alternative: Group members could pair off and ask one another these questions as an "interview."

Family Ties

The moment our life begins, we become part of the human race, one of over five billion people around the world. It's pretty hard to relate to billions of people. (Imagine the phone bill!) But we have a closer connection. We belong to a family.

● **How would you define** *family*?

_____

● **Who are the people in your family?**

_____

● **What makes all of you a family?**

_____

Our last name can provide additional information about who we are. It connects us to a family with a history and a special heritage. Growing up, we learn about our family and add to the story as we live out our own lives.

● **How did you get your last name?**

_____

● **Does your last name have an ethnic connection? What?**

_____

_____

● **Does your last name mean or stand for something? What?**

_____

_____

_____

2

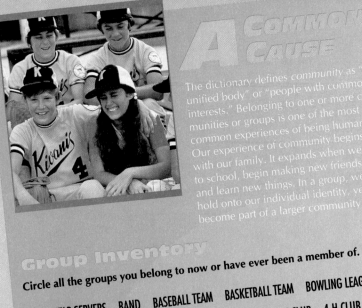

A Common Cause

The dictionary defines *community* as "a unified body" or "people with common interests." Belonging to one or more communities or groups is one of the most common experiences of being human. Our experience of community begins with our family. It expands when we go to school, begin making new friends, and learn new things. In a group, we hold onto our individual identity, yet become part of a larger community.

Group Inventory

Circle all the groups you belong to now or have ever been a member of.

ALTAR SERVERS   BAND   BASEBALL TEAM   BASKETBALL TEAM   BOWLING LEAGUE

C.Y.O.   CHEERLEADERS   CHOIR   DANCE CLASS   FAN CLUB   4-H CLUB

JUNIOR HIGH SCHOOL   MIDDLE SCHOOL   OUTDOORS CLUB   SCHOOL NEWSPAPER

SCIENCE CLUB   SCOUTS   SOCCER TEAM   SOFTBALL TEAM   STUDENT COUNCIL

SUMMER CAMP   SWIM TEAM   TRACK TEAM   YOUTH GROUP

List some groups not included above.

_____

_____

What are some of the benefits of belonging to a group?

_____

_____

_____

_____

Move on to "Family Ties," on page 2. After the group members have quietly read and answered the three questions about their families, brainstorm together a group definition of *family*. Write this definition on the chalkboard or chart paper.

You may ask volunteers to share their answers to the three questions, but be sensitive to the variety of family situations that may exist among the members of your group. Do not require that everyone respond.

Repeat the same procedure for the questions about last names at the end of that section.

Alternative: Leave the questions about last names as an exercise the young people can finish at home and share with the group during the next session. This approach will involve their families in the session and allow them to see how the group is starting out.

Exploring   (20 minutes)

After the participants read "A Common Cause," have them complete the "Group Inventory." Keep a list on the chalkboard or chart paper to find out whether any of the young people belong to similar groups. It might be interesting to discover, if some are in the same club or group, how their opinions of that group differ or agree. After completing the inventory, allow the discussion to flow about the benefits and responsibilities of belonging to a group.

Optional Activity   *You may extend the session by adding the following activity.*

Find and preview a video that portrays an organization (perhaps one that is listed in the "Group Inventory"). It might be part of a team's game or a project some school or community organization completed. Show this to the group and then invite group members to discuss the possible pros and cons of belonging to this organization.

Me, Myself, and God

What about religion? Is it something private that we keep to ourselves, or is it something we share with others? Most people would say that it's both.

Our relationship with God is special because it's personal. It's the most personal relationship we have. God knows, loves, and cares for every person on earth. God calls each of us by name. But there are two sides to every relationship. We respond to God's love by believing in and praying to God.

God calls each of us not only as individuals, but as members of a community. People of every era and culture have discovered that their faith in God is strengthened when they share it with others. Some of the religions that have developed around the world include Hinduism, Buddhism, Judaism, Christianity, and Islam. Each of these religions represents a community's response to a divine call.

3

Next, ask everyone to complete the "Personality Profile" on page 3. Group members should not be made to share their results with the others, but you could ask general questions such as, "Were you surprised at the results of this profile?"

It is important to note that there is nothing scientific about this survey and it would be unfair for people to be made to feel stereotyped by the results. The goal is to help everyone uncover some aspects of his or her personality and see how life offers opportunities to expand and explore other sides of life.

Alternative: If the group members seem comfortable with one another, pair off "loners" with those who prefer group activity. Ask them to talk with each other about their responses to the "Personality Profile."

After asking the members of the group to quietly read "Me, Myself, and God," present to them the idea of religion as having both a personal and a communal dimension. You may wish to discuss religion and faith in general terms, as a common feature of most human cultures, or talk about some specific world religions the group members may be familiar with.

Jesus' Faith

In these sessions, we'll be taking a look at how the Catholic Christian community started and grew. It began with Jesus. As a member of the Jewish religion, Jesus lived and worshipped in a community of faith. He also spent time praying on his own.

Jesus' words and actions helped others know of God's love for them. He gathered together a group of disciples who became a community of believers. The Catholic Church traces its history back to these first Christians, whose stories can be found in the Christian Scriptures, or New Testament.

Our Parish Family

When we belong to a *parish*, a local Catholic faith community, we try to live as members of a family. We pray together, especially at Mass, and we celebrate special occasions together. We help one another, particularly the poor and the sick. We teach others about Jesus. Through these experiences, our parish family grows in the love of God and one another.

A parish joins many small families into a larger family—a community of faith—where we try to make Jesus' message of love come alive. We can do that because we put aside all our personal names and take on the name *Christian*, joining together in the name of Jesus Christ.

4

Parish Scorecard

Let's see how much of a family your parish community is. On a scale of 1 (rarely) to 5 (always), rate your parish on these characteristics.

	1 2 3 4 5
When I go to church, I see people of all ages.	1 2 3 4 5
Many people help at Mass by leading the singing, reading from the Scriptures, and giving out communion.	1 2 3 4 5
There are always many activities, meetings, and events going on at my parish.	1 2 3 4 5
The parish staff tries to get to know everyone.	1 2 3 4 5
People at church are generally friendly.	1 2 3 4 5
Our parish helps people who are poor, lonely, or sick.	1 2 3 4 5
People my age are treated as an important part of my parish.	1 2 3 4 5

Name two ways your parish could become more of a family.

_____

_____

Name two ways you could help.

_____

_____

Focus the group's attention on the origins of the Catholic Christian community by asking a volunteer to read aloud "Jesus' Faith," on page 4.

Alternative: The group members may themselves be able to describe the origins of the Catholic Church. If so, elicit this information from them rather than asking them to read this section.

3 Connecting (15 minutes)

Talking about the participants' experience of Church and parish can serve as an introduction to "Our Parish Family." Before they read this material, you may wish to point out that parishes, made up of imperfect human beings, do not always live up to the ideal described in this section.

Completing the "Parish Scorecard" exercise will allow the young people to share their opinions about their local

parish. It is important to provide some means of communicating the group's suggestions to parish leadership, and to help the young people get more involved in working towards improving the parish.

Distribute markers and sheets of chart paper. Ask the group members, in teams or pairs, to describe, with words and pictures, the "ideal" parish. They might consider the leadership, the works (community service, educational, social, and recreational) to be carried out, the worship, and even the design of the church building and other parish facilities. Share these descriptions with the rest of the group.

Gather the young people together for prayer. Ask a volunteer to read the description of the early Christian community in Acts 2:42–47. Close by inviting each person to pray (aloud or silently) for the Church and all of its members.

CHARACTERISTICALLY CATHOLIC

FOCUS

Certain beliefs and practices are associated with the Catholic Church.

Objectives

To help the participants:
- become aware of the common beliefs of Christian communities;
- understand some basic beliefs and practices of the Roman Catholic Church;
- know the four marks of the Church.

Materials Needed

Bible • pens/pencils • copies of the diocesan newspaper • four candles and matches • parish bulletins (for the Optional Activity)

Session Outline

Breaking the Ice (10 minutes)
- "Show and tell" personal items that identify the group members.

1. Starting Out (10 minutes)
- Read "One in a Billion" and identify various Christian communities.
- Share stories of how group members became Catholic Christians.
- Complete a "Baptism Data Card."

2. Exploring (30 minutes)
- Note some beliefs that Christians share in "All in the Family."
- Name and define the sacraments in "Seven Signs of God's Love."
- Learn about the Church hierarchy ("In the Apostles' Footsteps").
- Discuss the saints and Mary ("Special People" and "Mother of the Church").
- Explore religious orders of men and women in "Witnesses to the Kingdom."

3. Connecting (10 minutes)
- Reflect on the four marks of the Church.
- Pray for the Church, its leaders, and all of its members.
- Optional Activity: You may extend the session by adding the Optional Activity.

Breaking the Ice

Ask each young person to check his or her pockets, purses, or wallets for some personal item that represents and identifies him or her. Sitting in a circle, invite each participant to show the item and explain what it says about him or her.

Alternative: Group members could describe items they have in their rooms or lockers.

Who Am I?

How often do we ask ourselves that question? And how often does the answer change? Probably each time. That's because we change. But in spite of it, there's a constant that defines us. There are choices we make and have made that carve out an identity for us.

Adolescents begin to take responsibility for their image and personality. They define themselves by what they like or dislike, get involved with, do, wear, listen to, and on and on. All of this is very fluid and will emerge, change, and redefine numerous times. That's part of the fun of being young: to explore and try new things. Helping them understand this process will help them to also see how we shape up as a Catholic Church.

Giving young people an appreciation for the Church means helping them see that while the Church changes, there are also constants that define it. The doctrine and beliefs we share have evolved through the ages but are centered around what is called a "deposit of faith." That phrase may sound cold and dry, but our faith started out in a totally different fashion.

Symbols Speak

The fish is one of the most basic symbols of Christianity. We know that Christians used to draw the fish symbol to identify themselves to other Christians lest they divulge their identity. Learning about the faith was a matter of doing and living, not studying and memorizing. "They went to the temple area together every day, while in their homes they broke bread. With exultant and sincere hearts they took their meals in common, praising God . . ." (Acts 2:46–47).

Catholic Christianity is rich in symbolism. Bread and wine, light, water, oil. All these basic elements speak volumes. However, we often dull them with words and pronouncements instead of having them draw us into their deep meaning.

An important way to help young people appreciate the Church's identity is to discover and explore what these symbols are and how they bond us into community. Walking into a church and just studying the stained glass can reveal volumes of meaning. Observing what takes place at a baptism reveals the essence of Christianity.

Living History

We believe our faith is shaped by Scripture and tradition. While much may be found in the Bible, other faith essentials have developed in response to crises in the Church at different times. This approach distinguishes the Catholic community from other Christian denominations. Unity in the pope, reverence for Mary, the Mother of Jesus, devotion to saints as models of Christian living are particularly associated with Catholicism.

Christian religions, however, share much in common: Jesus is the Messiah who has saved us, the Bible is the inspired word of God, and the Eucharist is a gathering of the faithful. An exciting development in ecumenism is the common work or service to the poor. Many congregations bond together in these important ventures.

Young people may appreciate the Catholic Christian call to believe, accept, live, and love. Believe in Jesus as our Savior, accept the presence of Jesus in our worship, live in community founded in Jesus' name, and love as Jesus did. That comes pretty close to the spirit of the early Christians.

Reflections

1. What is the most important characteristic I attribute to the Catholic Church?
2. Have I noticed change in the Church and how do I feel about it?
3. Do any Church symbols speak powerfully to me?

2 CHARACTERISTICALLY CATHOLIC

One in a Billion

Are you one in a billion? When it comes to religion, you could say so. As a Christian, you are one of about 1.78 billion Christians around the world. Some Christian communities you may have heard of include Episcopalians, Lutherans, Eastern Orthodox, Roman Catholics, Baptists, Methodists, and Presbyterians.

As a Roman Catholic Christian, you're also one of about a billion Catholics worldwide. How did you get to be a Catholic Christian?

BAPTISM DATA CARD

I, _____,

WAS BAPTIZED ON _____,

IN _____

_____ CHURCH.

MY GODPARENTS ARE _____

AND _____.

All in the Family

You may wonder how so many different groups can all be Christian. It's not unlike a large family where the brothers and sisters grow up, take on different careers, and end up living all over the country, raising their own families. In the same way, all of these faith communities share the same last name—Christian—and a common heritage, but each has its own unique first name, with its own special history, characteristics, and customs.

Some of the beliefs and traditions of the various Christian communities are similar; many are different. These differences sometimes have led to disagreements. In this century, many Christian communities have begun to talk together about what we share and what we agree on.

Some beliefs that Christians share are that there are three Persons in one God (the Trinity), that Jesus is the Son of God, our Savior, that the Bible is the inspired word of God, and that Baptism gives us a share in God's life. Another important area of agreement is Jesus' call for all Christians to help and serve others. Many churches work together to feed the hungry or provide shelter for the homeless.

5

---

1 Starting Out (10 minutes)

Ask a volunteer to read the first paragraph of "One in a Billion" on page 5. Have the group members look closely at the names of the various Christian communities. What, if anything, do they know about any of them? Can they add any other Christian communities to this list?

Another volunteer can read the remaining paragraph. Ask each participant to think about the way he or she became a Catholic Christian. Encourage group members to share their stories or memories.

Give the group members some time to complete the "Baptism Data Card." (Many young people won't be able to fill in all of the information without some help from home. Encourage them to talk to parents, godparents, and other relatives about their baptism.)

Stress that however one becomes a Catholic, what's important is the way in which we live our belief.

2 Exploring (30 minutes)

Ask one or two group members to read aloud "All in the Family." Review any questions or comments about similarities and differences among the various Christian communities. Encourage the participants to find the answers to any questions they might have, either through library research or by contacting other churches. You might also be able to invite a guest speaker from a local Christian community.

Finally, ask the youths to describe, if possible, local situations in which different churches have worked together: feeding the hungry, staffing a used clothing store, and so on. You could even plan a group project with young people from another Christian church.

CATHOLIC BELIEFS

In this session, we'll be looking at some of the beliefs and practices that are especially associated with the Catholic Church. These are ways that we live out our faith as Catholic Christians.

Seven Signs of God's Love

Special moments are celebrated by the Catholic Church in rituals called *sacraments*. A sacrament is a sacred sign that celebrates God's love for us and Jesus' presence in our lives and in the Church. We'll be taking a closer look at the sacraments a little later. For now, unscramble the names of the seven sacraments and match them with their descriptions.

LOYH DROSER   NYMORTIMA   THUSCAERI   TRINCOFIMANO ✳

NINIGANOT FO HET KICS   SMIPTAB   NICCORELIANTOI

1. _____ welcomes us into the Christian community and cleanses us from original sin.

2. _____ strengthens the presence of the Holy Spirit, which we first received at Baptism.

3. _____ celebrates Jesus' real presence in the consecrated bread and wine we share.

4. _____ grants us God's mercy and forgiveness of our sins.

5. _____ asks Jesus to bring healing, comfort and strength to those who are seriously ill.

6. _____ proclaims a man's and a woman's lifelong promise of mutual love and commitment.

7. _____ ordains men to serve the Church as deacons, priests, or bishops.

6

Introduce the material on pages 6 and 7 with a look at "Catholic Beliefs" on page 6. Point out to the young people that this session will concentrate on four specific topics within the Catholic Church.

- the seven sacraments ("Seven Signs of God's Love")
- the hierarchy ("In the Apostles' Footsteps")
- the saints and Mary ("Special People" and "Mother of the Church")
- religious orders ("Witnesses to the Kingdom")

Divide the participants into four smaller groups, and assign each group one of these topics. Instruct them to read and discuss their section, then prepare a "mini-lesson" that will present this information to the other group members in a creative way.

Give the smaller groups time to prepare their lessons, then ask them, one at a time, to teach their material to the other participants.

You may need to spend more or less time on each section, depending on the backgrounds of the group members. There is no need, however, to go into great detail on every topic in this one session. If necessary, you can spend some time on basic Catholic beliefs in the remaining sessions.

✳ 1. Baptism; 2. Confirmation; 3. Eucharist; 4. Reconciliation; 5. Anointing of the Sick; 6. Matrimony; 7. Holy Orders

In the Apostles' Footsteps

The pope, as bishop of Rome and successor of the apostle Peter, is the leader of the Catholic Church. He represents the unity of Roman Catholics throughout the world. In union with the pope are the bishops, who oversee *dioceses*, local groups of parishes.

Do you know the name of your diocese? Do you know who your bishop is? Who is the pope?

On a smaller scale is the parish community, usually led by a priest who serves as pastor. The pastor and many other men and women are involved in the various parish ministries.

Who are some of the leaders in your parish? What are some parish organizations?

ONE PERSON WHOM I ADMIRE IS
_____
_____
BECAUSE _____
_____
_____
_____

SPECIAL PEOPLE

Christians believe that individuals who have lived lives of love, faith, and service live forever with God in heaven. We call these people *saints*. When the Catholic Church canonizes someone, or declares him or her a saint, it means we believe that the person shares eternal life with God and should be looked at as a model of Christian living. We pray to God through them, take their names in Baptism, and name cities, churches, and other institutions after them. We may also celebrate their feast days or own medals or statues of our patron saints.

Not all saints are famous or well-known, however. Anyone who puts God first in his or her life may be a saint. You may know someone whom you consider to be a saint because of his or her faith and good deeds. In fact, you or one of your friends may someday be canonized as a saint!

For the section, "In the Apostles' Footsteps," on page 7, you may wish to review the institutional structure and offices of the Church. It would be helpful to focus on the local Catholic community, especially on the diocesan level. If possible, bring in copies of the diocesan newspaper, which may contain a photo of your local bishop. This may help the group members feel more a part of the larger Catholic community.

Alternative: Invite the pastor, parish administrator, or president of the parish council to talk about the history, organization, and leadership of your parish.

In dealing with the material in "Special People," remind the group members that every Christian is called to live as a saint, a person who puts God first in his or her life. Invite the young people to name those people whom they especially admire, explaining the reasons for their admiration.

You may also ask the group members to talk about or do some research on any saints that especially interest them.

Stained glass window, Goa, India

MOTHER OF THE CHURCH

Mary, the mother of Jesus, has a special role in the Church. She is honored above all other saints as the mother of God. The Gospels mention Mary several times. John's Gospel recalls that Mary was with Jesus at Cana as the first believer in his mission. She was by his side at the crucifixion. She was with the disciples after the resurrection and received the Holy Spirit with them at Pentecost. We look to Mary as the model of a true disciple of Jesus.

Mary was a strong woman of faith, trust, and compassion. She lived as her son lived, in the service of God and people. She lived perfectly the life of faith that all Jesus' followers are called to live. Catholics look to Mary as the mother of the Church. We ask her to help us respond to God's call.

What do you know about these feast days honoring Mary?

Annunciation *(March 25)*

Assumption *(August 15)*

Immaculate Conception *(December 8)*

Witnesses to the Kingdom

All Catholic Christians are called to live lives of faith, prayer, community, and service. Some Catholics decide to live these Gospel values as members of a religious community. These men (called *priests* or *brothers*) and women (called *nuns* or *sisters*) do not marry. They may work at a variety of ministries, such as teaching or parish work. They make vows of poverty, chastity, and obedience. Religious communities of men and women have existed in the Church for hundreds of years. Three you may have heard of are the Franciscans, the Jesuits, and the Dominicans.

What are some reasons a person might decide to join a religious order?

_____

_____

_____

_____

_____

Marks of the Church

Leader: Lord, we are your Church, called to unity. Though conflicts and divisions exist, we strive for unity and harmony among all your people.

All: Jesus, help us to be one.

Leader: Lord, we are your Church, called to holiness. Though we are sinful, we strive to learn your will and be open to your presence.

All: Jesus, help us to be holy.

Leader: Lord, we are your Church, called to be open to all. In spite of our prejudices, we strive to bring your good news to all people, for this is the true meaning of our name, *catholic*.

All: Jesus, help us to be universal.

Leader: Lord, we are your Church, called to be faithful to the apostles' teaching. In spite of differences, we strive to remain faithful to the traditions of apostolic teaching and service.

All: Jesus, help us to be apostolic.

After a look at the section, "Mother of the Church," on page 8, ask volunteers to explain the feast days honoring Mary. You may wish to discuss other feast days as well, particularly local or cultural devotions.

The section "Witnesses to the Kingdom" discusses religious orders of men and women. If possible, invite a nun, priest, or brother to talk about the history and ministry of his or her order, as well as his or her reasons for entering religious life.

3 Connecting (10 minutes)

Designate a group member to lead the prayer, "Marks of the Church," on page 8. Gather the group members together, sitting in a circle. In the center of the group arrange four candles, to represent the four marks of the Church.

As the leader reads each section, ask one young person to light one candle. Briefly discuss with the group members some ways that Catholics, as individuals and as a community, can live according to that mark of the Church.

Close with a period of prayer, aloud or silent, for the Church, its leaders, and all of its members.

Optional Activity *You may extend the session by adding the following activity.*

Distribute a copy of the parish bulletin to each participant. Ask everyone to look in the bulletin to find evidence of each of the four marks of the Church. You might consider bringing in bulletins from several weekends, which would give a better sense of the variety of church services and activities.

FOCUS

Sacraments
celebrate God's
love and
Jesus' presence
in our lives.

LET'S CELEBRATE!

Objectives

To help the participants:
- appreciate God's presence in the special and routine moments of our lives;
- understand the seven sacraments;
- connect the sacraments with experiences of welcoming, forgiving, and helping one another in daily life.

Materials Needed

chart paper/marker or chalkboard/chalk (for Breaking the Ice) • Bibles (at least four) • paper and pens/pencils • ten preprinted sheets of paper and a container (for the Optional Activity) • candle and matches

Session Outline

Breaking the Ice   (10 minutes)
- Describe a fictional sport.

1. Starting Out   (15 minutes)
- Reflect on some "Milestones of Life."
- Consider the sacraments as "Milestones of Faith."
- Participate in a Scripture search on Catholic symbols.

2. Exploring   (25 minutes)
- Read "Sacraments of Initiation" and discuss the sacraments of Baptism, Confirmation, and Eucharist.
- Read "Sacraments of Healing" and discuss the sacraments of Reconciliation and Anointing of the Sick.
- Optional Activity: You may extend the session by adding the Optional Activity.
- Read "Sacraments of Commitment" and discuss the sacraments of Matrimony and Holy Orders.

3. Connecting   (10 minutes)
- Write and share prayers in "Everyday God."
- Think of ways we can live the sacraments in our everyday lives.

Breaking the Ice

Ask the group to simulate a team that plays a sport called "floofing." Invite the young people to describe this fictional sport. How is it played? Are uniforms worn? What equipment is necessary? What are the rules? Use the chalkboard or chart paper to map out this sport. Next, ask the participants to describe how someone would make the floofing team. What qualities would the candidate need to display in tryouts? Once someone makes the team, how would he or she advance? What abilities would make someone a star player? What would an M.V.F. (Most Valuable Floofer) have to achieve?

Background for Session 3

Real Rituals

Thanksgiving dinner, birthday parties, graduation ceremonies. These are rituals most people go through without ever thinking of them as scripted and programmed. Yet, there are common threads that make these rituals comforting in their predictability. They mark important celebrations and gatherings in the lives of almost everyone. Maybe, the post-50-year-olds don't want to be reminded of approaching "senioritis." Most people, however, like to hear "Happy Birthday" and enjoy blowing out candles on a cake.

As a community, the Church marks special turning points in life—birth, adolescence, marriage, reconciliation, sickness, service, and community participation—with rituals known as sacraments. These originate in one way or the other from the New Testament, though in differing ways. Baptism and Eucharist are mentioned specifically. Other sacraments are derived from acts of Jesus.

The Church celebrates sacraments as signs of God's presence in the community. They are rituals that do not so much exact conformity as ensure continuity through time and in different locations. The last decades have witnessed changes in sacramental celebrations to highlight the communal aspect of the celebration and to tie them to the Eucharist, the most basic sacrament.

Signs of Life

There are universal symbols that people recognize and understand—the Red Cross for first aid, a cigarette with a line through it that means do not smoke. The liturgy or public worship of the Church employs symbols, which speak volumes, in the sacramental rituals.

Bread and wine at the Eucharist can be seen as food and drink and also as elements mentioned at the Last Supper. They also symbolize the presence of Jesus and, in a larger way, stand for the community of believers. The breaking of bread shows how the people find unity in each other assembled as one.

Oil, fire, water, the laying on of hands, the exchange of rings, are common symbols found in sacramental celebrations, and they relate to the Paschal Mystery—the dying and rising of Jesus. It is best to let the symbols speak for themselves, since Catholics sometimes cover over gestures and signs with words.

Making Connections

Sacraments are community builders. They exhort us to be attentive to these key moments in life and call upon the community to support and celebrate the persons involved. It's just like the accolades a town showers on its winning baseball team. There'll be a parade, photos in the local newspapers, presentation of trophies by the mayor. The star athletes bring honor to the community, which lets the young people know how much they're appreciated.

The sacramental groupings: initiation, healing, and commitment, speak to the fundamental experiences of life. Joining and belonging to community, reconciling differences in the interest of unity, and developing relationships are experiences that bond people together in common endeavors. The Church celebrates sacraments to help individuals see each other as brothers and sisters.

Reflections

1. What's your favorite ritual in life and how does it make you feel to celebrate it?
2. Can you remember the celebration of a particular sacrament that was particularly moving? What made it so?
3. Why do you think even the most alienated Catholics often want to have their child baptized?

3 Let's Celebrate!

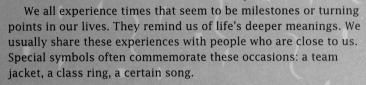
"Sometimes you get to a point in
your life when you just have to stop
and think about what it all means.
You realize that there's more to life
than just getting through the day."

Look at the photos and imagine
yourself in each situation. Then
write a brief reflection for each.

Milestones of Life

We all experience times that seem to be milestones or turning
points in our lives. They remind us of life's deeper meanings. We
usually share these experiences with people who are close to us.
Special symbols often commemorate these occasions: a team
jacket, a class ring, a certain song.

On the other hand, much of life tends to follow a pretty predictable pattern. But that doesn't make it insignificant. Because
we're made in the image and likeness of God, our Creator, our
lives have special meaning and significance. They are sacred.

Jesus, the Son of God, revealed the sacredness of our lives
when he became one of us and shared our existence. He experienced the routine and the special, the sad and the happy. He
showed us that God is with us at every moment in our journey
through life.

Milestones of Faith

As Catholics, we share our journey with others who believe in
Jesus. Together, we celebrate God's presence with us. The seven
sacraments are the Catholic Church community's principal ways of
celebrating our journey through life. When we celebrate the sacraments, we gather together as a community of believers. In a powerful way, we acknowledge God's love for us and Jesus' presence in
our lives and in the Church. With the community, we experience
that love and presence in the celebration of the sacraments and
we ask for that love and presence to continue in our lives.

9

Starting Out (15 minutes)

Ask the group members to read quietly the quote
printed above the section, "Milestones of Life," on
page 9 of the YOUTH MAGAZINE, and look carefully at the
three photos on that page. Distribute paper and pens or
pencils and ask the young people to write a brief
reflection or caption for each photo. When everyone is
finished, invite volunteers to read their reflections to the
group.

Next, ask one or two volunteers to read aloud the rest of
that section. Based on the photos and their reading,
brainstorm a list of other turning points in life. Talk
about the symbols or objects often associated with these
important milestones. Invite the participants to reflect on
what have been some of the turning points in their own
lives. (Do not require that anyone share these personal
memories.) Remind the group that even our most routine
activities have meaning and significance because of
Jesus' presence in our lives.

Alternative: Group members could role-play several of
these turning points.

Introduce the seven sacraments by asking a volunteer to
read "Milestones of Faith" at the bottom of the page.
Review with the group the definition of *sacrament* and
the reasons that Catholics celebrate the sacraments.

Note that some groups may be less familiar with this
material, and may need to spend more time going over
the basic facts about the sacraments. Other groups may
be ready to treat the sacraments in more depth by
concentrating on the meanings behind the actions,
words, and symbols.

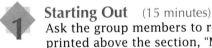

Sacraments of Initiation

When we become part of a group, we gain an identity as a member of a larger community. Think about the groups you belong to. How are new members welcomed? What do you do to build a spirit of togetherness?

We become part of the Church through the three sacraments of initiation: Baptism, Confirmation, and Eucharist. These sacraments prepare us to follow Jesus in the world as members of the Catholic Church. New adult members celebrate all three sacraments of initiation together (usually during the Easter Vigil), though many Catholics celebrate them separately at different times in their lives.

BAPTISM

Through the waters of Baptism, which represent life and death, we share in Jesus' death and resurrection. The water, *chrism* (holy oil), white garment, and lighted candle of Baptism symbolize dying to sin and rising to new life in the body of Christ. Baptism welcomes us into the Christian Community, frees us from all sin, including original sin, and unites us with Jesus.

CONFIRMATION

Confirmation reaffirms our baptismal promises and renews our commitment to the Catholic faith. We express our faith for ourselves and accept our responsibilities as followers of Jesus. The Holy Spirit, received in Baptism and strengthened in Confirmation, helps us to live as witnesses of Jesus in the world. During the celebration, the bishop or priest lays his hand on the head of the one to be confirmed and anoints the forehead with chrism. These actions seal us with the gift of the Holy Spirit and signify our participation in Christ's ministry.

EUCHARIST

The Eucharist unites us with Jesus and the Church. The community gathers to recall Jesus' Last Supper and celebrate the gift of his life and presence among us. We eat and drink the consecrated bread and wine which are Jesus' body and blood, his very life shared with us. We go into the world to serve God by helping others. Through us, Jesus reaches out to meet all of the world's hungers.

10

Divide the young people into smaller groups for a Scripture search. Assign one or two symbols to each group. The group members should read their Scripture passage, then answer this question: "What can this symbol mean for the faith life of someone my age?"

Scripture passages: Mark 14:22–24 (bread and wine); Luke 3:16 (water and fire); Acts 8:17–19 (laying on of hands); 1 Samuel 16:13 (anointing with oil).

Alternative: Display a lighted candle, containers of water, wine, and oil, and a loaf of bread on a table. Invite the participants to talk about the everyday uses of each item. Then discuss the special symbolism of each item as a sign of one of the sacraments.

Exploring (20 minutes)
Ask a volunteer to read the first paragraph of "Sacraments of Initiation" on page 10. Talk briefly with the young people about how various groups

welcome new members and build a spirit of togetherness. Encourage volunteers to share stories of personal experiences.

Follow this discussion by reading the rest of "Sacraments of Initiation." (Relate this material to Breaking the Ice, if your group did that activity.) Talk about the process that enables a person to grow in the love of Jesus, to come to the Lord's table, and to live his or her life as a committed Catholic.

Continue the exploration of the sacraments of initiation by reading and reviewing together the descriptions of the sacraments of Baptism, Confirmation, and Eucharist. Encourage group members to share personal experiences of celebrating or attending any of the sacraments of initiation, describing what they observed, felt, and experienced.

Sacraments of Healing

Relationships don't always run smoothly. We can hurt, and be hurt by, the people we're closest to. We offer our support to people who are going through rough times. How do you ask for, or offer, forgiveness? How can you help those who are suffering?

God wants us to be at peace within ourselves, with God, and with each other. In order to experience such peace, the Church celebrates the sacraments of healing: Reconciliation and the Anointing of the Sick. These sacraments bring us the peace and presence of Jesus.

RECONCILIATION

When we sin, we make a conscious choice to turn away from God and one another. Through the sacrament of Reconciliation, we can experience a *conversion*, a turning back, to God and the Church community. We talk to the priest about what we've done wrong, expressing our sorrow and our willingness to change. The priest blesses us and says the words of absolution, forgiving our sins in the name of Jesus and the Church.

ANOINTING OF THE SICK

The Anointing of the Sick brings Jesus' healing, comfort, and strength to those who are seriously ill, elderly, or in danger of death. During the celebration, the priest anoints the person with oil and prays for forgiveness, healing, and strength of mind and body. Sometimes Jesus brings physical healing through this sacrament. He always brings love, strength, and support to the sick person and to his or her loved ones.

11

Next, ask everyone to quietly read the first paragraph of "Sacraments of Healing," on page 11. Elicit responses to the questions at the end of that paragraph. Encourage volunteers to share stories of personal experiences.

Divide the participants into smaller groups of three or four people. Ask each group to come up with a situation that involves making up or reconciliation. Once they have created a scenario, ask them to write the dialogue that reveals the reconciliation. Recruit volunteers who are willing to act out their dialogues for the others.

Afterwards, finish reading the rest of "Sacraments of Healing." Continue the exploration of the sacraments of healing by reading and reviewing together the descriptions of the sacraments of Reconciliation and Anointing of the Sick. Participants may be able to share personal experiences of celebrating or attending one of these sacraments.

Optional Activity   *You may extend the session by adding the following activity.*

In preparation, label ten sheets of paper: LOVE, ACCOMPLISHMENT, DEATH, PEACE, SORROW, FRIENDSHIP, ANGER, PRIDE, HOPE, FAITH. Fold the sheets and place them in a container. Divide the group equally into two teams, A and B.

One member of Team A chooses a paper and has 30 seconds to think of something that symbolizes that concept. Using the chalkboard or chart paper, the person draws the symbol, and the other members of Team A have one minute to guess the concept being symbolized. (The person drawing cannot give hints.) Team B then does the same, and the two teams alternate until all the concepts have been covered.

Sacraments of Commitment

Faithfulness is a quality we look for in each of our relationships. When have you shown loyalty to the people you care about by standing by those who need your presence?

In the sacraments of commitment, the Church celebrates two ways that men and women serve others by sharing their gifts and their presence. These sacraments are Matrimony and Holy Orders.

MATRIMONY

Matrimony celebrates the lifelong love of a man and woman for each other. Their vows express the *covenant*, or special bond of love, between the husband and wife, who administer the sacrament to one another in the presence of the priest or deacon and the entire community as witnesses. The wedding rings, blessed by the priest, are symbols of this covenant.

In marriage, a man and a woman share in God's life-giving power and become one. Often their love brings forth children. Through their unselfish love and care for their children, parents are a living sign of God's love and mercy.

HOLY ORDERS

All who are baptized share in the ministry and priesthood of Jesus. Some are called to share in Jesus' ministry in the sacrament of Holy Orders. In this sacrament, bishops, priests, and deacons are ordained to serve the Catholic community.

The word *ordain* means "to set aside." Priests are ordained by a bishop to help him in ministering to the Church. They work in parishes, schools, hospitals—wherever there is a need to bring God's love to others. Deacons care for the needy in the community. They may also baptize, proclaim the Gospel at Mass, witness marriages, and preside at funerals. The word *deacon* means "helper" or "server."

12

Everyday God

The risen Jesus continues to speak and act in our daily experiences and in world events through the people who make up his Church. Catholic Christians are called to live the sacraments every day by welcoming and joining with others (initiation), forgiving one another (healing), and helping those who need it (commitment). How can you live the sacraments in your daily life?

* in school
* at home
* with friends
* on a team
* in a club
* in the community

Write a prayer asking God to help you be a sign—a sacrament—of Jesus' presence in your everyday life.

_____
_____
_____
_____
_____
_____
_____

After the group members read the first paragraph of "Sacraments of Commitment," on page 12, begin a brief discussion on the importance of faithfulness and loyalty in any relationship. As a group, come up with a list of characteristics of the perfect friend or family member. (Be sensitive to group members who may be living with difficult family situations.)

Ask a volunteer to read aloud the rest of "Sacraments of Commitment." Continue the exploration of the sacraments of commitment by reviewing together the sacraments of Matrimony and Holy Orders. Participants may be able to share personal experiences of attending the celebration of one of these sacraments.

Next, brainstorm together two lists: one describing characteristics of the perfect husband or wife, and another describing the perfect bishop, priest, or deacon. Compare these lists with the list describing the perfect friend or family member created earlier.

Connecting (15 minutes)

Create an atmosphere for prayer by gathering everyone into a circle and lighting a candle at the center of the group. After a volunteer reads aloud "Everyday God," ask everyone to write a prayer in the space provided. Spend some time talking with the group about ways we, as Catholics, can live the sacraments in our everyday lives by welcoming, forgiving, and helping one another. Encourage them to mention some specific actions they can take in their own lives.

Close by inviting volunteers to share their prayers.

FOCUS

The Eucharist
is a
meal
of
thanksgiving.

GIVING THANKS

Objectives

To help the participants:
- understand the Liturgy of the Word as the sharing of stories of the Christian community;
- appreciate the Liturgy of the Eucharist as the sharing of a meal in remembrance of Jesus:
- reflect on reasons for attending Mass.

Materials Needed

snacks and other party supplies (for Breaking the Ice) • Bible (or Lectionary) • pens/pencils and paper • chart paper/marker (or chalk board/chalk) • loaf of soft-crusted bread

Session Outline

Breaking the Ice   (15 minutes)
- Celebrate with an informal get-together.

1. Starting Out   (10 minutes)
- Read and discuss a story about "A Family Tradition."
- Optional Activity: You may extend the session by adding the Optional Activity.
- Share memories of "Talk Around the Table."

2. Exploring   (20 minutes)
- Summarize the two parts of the celebration of the Eucharist.
- Read "Sharing Our Story" and review the Liturgy of the Word.
- In pairs, write petitions for the Prayer of the Faithful.
- Read "Sharing a Meal" and review the Liturgy of the Eucharist.

3. Connecting   (15 minutes)
- Discuss the question, "Why Go to Mass?"
- Role-play a parish Liturgy Committee meeting.
- List suggestions to improve the parish's liturgy.
- Share a Gospel reading and a loaf of bread.

Breaking the Ice

Arrange an informal get-together for the group members, which could include snacks (perhaps do-it-yourself ice cream sundaes or mini-pizzas), music, activities, and so on. Invite the participants to socialize, talk together, and simply "hang out."

Alternative: Use this time to plan with the group a more elaborate social gathering for some time in the next few weeks. Ask volunteers to take responsibility for the various items needed for the get-together: food, music, paper products, activities, clean-up, and so on. (This should be a purely social, not an educational, gathering.)

Why Is This Day Any Different?

It appears to regular church-goers that Masses on days such as Christmas and Easter are packed. These days are unrivaled in attendance by other Sundays and holy days. Referring to people who seem to come to church only on special feasts, we ourselves at some time or other may have used the term *A&P Catholics,* the *A&P* standing for Ash Wednesday and Palm Sunday.

While it would be desirable to have the "A&P's" participate in the Eucharist every Sunday, it is a sign of that celebration's influence that people do attend on special days, even if on no others. By doing so, they witness—if hesitantly—to the fact that the Eucharist is central to our faith life as Catholics.

Our Celebration of Faith

We gather together at the Eucharist as a community of believers, following Jesus' Last Supper instruction: "Do this in memory of me." What we celebrate in Jesus' memory is twofold: his sharing bread and wine—transformed into his body and blood—with the disciples at that Last Supper as well as his sacrifice on the following day, the first Good Friday, when his body and blood were broken and shed on the cross.

The two main parts of the Mass, the Liturgy of the Word and the Liturgy of the Eucharist, serve to unite us with the Church's experience of Jesus' Paschal mystery. This experience is not time-bound; it instead spans past, present, and future. The accounts from Scripture tell us of God's relationship with people throughout history, especially God's relationship with us in Jesus. Our prayers, homily, petitions, and song reflect our struggles, hopes, and vision for today's faith community. Sharing in the one bread and the one cup, broken and poured out for many, calls us to become one in Jesus.

A Communal Focus

While our participation in the Eucharist is on an individual basis, the celebration has a communal focus. Such a focus can be seen in modern church architecture. Unlike Gothic cathedrals, which draw our eyes upward toward God in heaven, recently-built churches often seat the community in a circle, centering people's attention on one another, the presider, the Scripture, and on the altar, or table.

The dining area and table have traditionally been important objects and spaces in people's homes, whether apartment or house. By dining around the table with those we love (even if, at times, we don't particularly like them!) we learn about living. Likewise, celebrating the Eucharist as a community—that is, gathering around the table of the Lord—needs to be done regularly, so we can build a sense of family and unite as a faith community.

This having been said, we are forced to recognize as catechists and youth ministers that young people comprise an age group that seems to miss Mass regularly. Some of this may be explained by adolescent rebellion against authority and anything that parents might expect rather than a true rejection of faith. It may also mean that the liturgy's communal focus, a focus that is quite important among young people themselves, is less than perfect. A concrete solution might involve the young people participating in the Eucharist as a group. This may more readily meet younger adolescents' needs, particularly the need to relate to God through their peers and through adults with whom they're comfortable.

Reflections

1. On what occasion did I last participate in a Eucharist that I found moving? What made it so?
2. How could my parish enhance its own celebration of the Eucharist? What contribution could I make to this?
3. In what ways might I help the young people in my group grow in appreciation of Sunday Eucharist?

4 GIVING THANKS

A *Family Tradition*

Angela Sabatino loved doing what most people would consider a real chore: cooking Easter dinner for 45 people. The guests would include her six children, their spouses, eighteen grandchildren, four of their spouses, and ten great-grandchildren.

She would start weeks in advance by planning a menu and a shopping list. During Holy Week, she'd begin cleaning the house, preparing the traditional foods, and arranging every detail, right down to the color of the napkins. On Holy Saturday she would attend the Easter Vigil liturgy in the evening so she could get up early on Easter Sunday and finish the cooking.

Mrs. Sabatino greeted each person as he or she arrived. The house was crammed with tables and chairs to seat the large family. As everyone sat down for the meal, there would always be one empty chair next to her at the head table. And every year, before saying grace, Mrs. Sabatino would stand and tell the same story, explaining the empty chair.

When she was a little girl in Italy, her large family was poor but her father always taught them to be thankful for the little they had. At Easter, he would go out into the street and find someone who had no family or no place to go for dinner. He would invite that person into the house and seat the stranger next to him. This thankfulness became a family tradition.

Why do you think Mrs. Sabatino set the extra place?

_____

_____

If you were part of this family, what would you like best about Easter dinner? Why?

_____

_____

13

---

1 Starting Out (10 minutes)

Give the participants a few moments to quietly read "A Family Tradition," on page 13 of the YOUTH MAGAZINE, and answer the two questions at the end of that section.

Alternative: Volunteers could role-play this story.

When everyone is finished, invite volunteers to share their responses to the two questions. Encourage group members to also talk about their own families' meals, holidays, and get-togethers.

Optional Activity *You may extend the session by adding the following activity.*

Remind the young people that the word *Eucharist* means "thanksgiving." Create a litany of thanksgiving by asking the youth to each think of something or someone for which he or she is thankful. Go around the group and invite each person to name his or her person or thing aloud. The group members should then write their items on a sheet of chart paper or posterboard, which they also can decorate with drawings and pictures. Hang this poster in the meeting room or in the church.

Talk Around the Table

There's something special about sharing a meal with family or friends. The food doesn't have to be elaborate, as long as the company is friendly. The bond among the people around the table gets stronger because of the sharing. And it's not just food that's being shared. Mealtime can also be a time for exchanging conversations, memories, and stories.

When Mrs. Sabatino and her family share the holiday meal and the traditional story, something even more important is being communicated: a spirit of love and belonging. We don't have to wait for a holiday to do this. Sharing a meal and a good story with people we care about can make any day a special occasion.

What's the best get-together you can remember sharing with family or friends? What made it so special?

_____

_____

How would you put together a celebration for your family or friends?

_____

_____

List some of the things your celebration would include.

_____

_____

Sharing Our Story

The Mass, or Eucharist, is a similar gathering for our parish family. Each Sunday, Catholics gather at church to celebrate Mass. It's one of the special things we do to show we're Catholic Christians. At Mass, we celebrate our identity as a community. We recognize Jesus' presence in the people gathered to celebrate the Eucharist, in the word that is proclaimed, and in the priest who presides. Most importantly, we recognize Jesus' presence under the appearances of the bread and wine we share. The word *Eucharist* means "thanksgiving." During the Mass we praise and thank God for all our gifts, especially the gift of God's Son, Jesus.

As in many family gatherings, at Mass we share stories of our heritage as well as a special meal. In the Liturgy of the Word, the first part of the Mass, we listen to God's word proclaimed in Scripture. These stories connect us to the long tradition of the Catholic Church. In the homily, the priest or deacon explains the readings and encourages us to carry out the message of Jesus in our own lives. We believe Jesus continues to speak to us through the Scripture readings and the homily. Together, we respond to God's word in prayer and song.

In the Prayer of the Faithful, the parish community prays for the world and its leaders, for the Church, and for those in need. What are some of the needs you see in your world? Write a petition for each.

_____

_____

_____

14

Ask one or two volunteers to read "Talk Around the Table," on page 14. Divide the young people into smaller groups of three or four to work on the three questions at the end of that section. For the first question, each participant should share one memory with the other members of the group. (Do not force those who may be reluctant to participate.) For the other questions, ask each group to create a list of the items they'd include to make a celebration with family or friends special. When they are finished, each group can share its list with the others and note similarities and differences.

2 **Exploring** (20 minutes)
Point out to the group that the Eucharist (especially the Sunday Mass) is a special gathering for the parish family. Explain that the celebration of the Eucharist is divided into two parts: the Liturgy of the Word and the Liturgy of the Eucharist. Compare these

two parts of the Mass to the stories and meals shared during the family gatherings the group members discussed earlier.

The section "Sharing Our Story" provides information on the Liturgy of the Word, the first part of the Mass. Review this material with the group members, discussing any questions or comments they might have. (You may wish to go over the Scripture readings for the coming Sunday with the young people.)

The last paragraph of that section refers to the Prayer of the Faithful, petitions for people in the Church and in the world. Pair off the participants and ask the pairs to write one or more petitions based on the needs of their family, friends, neighbors, school, community, country, or the world in general. Save these petitions for the closing prayer.

Sharing a Meal

At the beginning of the Liturgy of the Eucharist, the second part of the Mass, we bring to the altar the bread and wine that will be used for the eucharistic meal. We present the bread and wine—and ourselves—as an offering to God from the community. During the Eucharistic Prayer, we praise and thank God for the gifts of creation, especially for Jesus' gift of himself in the Eucharist. We remember Jesus' Last Supper with his disciples and we celebrate his passion, death, and resurrection. We state our belief in Christ's death and resurrection and our hope in his coming again.

Catholics believe that in the Eucharist, the consecrated bread and wine are Christ himself—his life, his body and blood. Without being changed in appearance, the bread and wine become Jesus' body and blood. We call this *transubstantiation.* When we receive Communion, we are united in a special way to Jesus, the Bread of Life, and to his Church—in our parish community and throughout the world.

15

The next section, "Sharing a Meal," on page 15, discusses the second part of the Mass: the Liturgy of the Eucharist. Review this material with the group members, discussing any questions or comments they might have. Remind them of the unity we share with Jesus and with the worldwide Church when we receive Communion.

Alternatives: You and the group members could plan to attend Mass together next weekend and share a snack afterwards. (Sitting with people they know may help the young people feel more a part of the parish.) Or, you could arrange for the group to celebrate a liturgy or Communion service, planned and led by the young people themselves. Families, friends, and other teens in the parish could be invited to this celebration.

3 Connecting (15 minutes)

Begin a discussion by asking the members of the group, "Why do Catholics go to Mass? Why do (or don't) <u>you</u> go to Mass?" Encourage everyone to express his or her honest opinions.

Why Go to Mass?

The Scene:
A Liturgy Committee meeting at Saint Aloysius parish. Several youth group members have been invited to help plan the Sunday liturgy.

The Characters:
Pat Carlson, chairperson of the Liturgy Committee
Father Howard, the pastor of Saint Aloysius
Agnes Brady, member of the Hospitality Ministry
Frank Zura, director of music
Mike Dabrowski, youth group member, age 14
Lorraine Machado, youth group member, age 13
C.J. Carbone, youth group member, age 13

Pat Carlson: Before we start talking about next Sunday's liturgy, let's see what everyone thought of last Sunday's Mass.

Lorraine Machado: I didn't go.

Frank Zura: What? You missed the choir's first performance!

C.J. Carbone: I went because my family's rule is that I have to go to Mass every Sunday until I'm 16.

Mike Dabrowski: Why do we have to go to church, anyway? You can pray to God just as well on your own.

16

Agnes Brady: Everyone should pray by themselves, but going to Mass is a way of joining with the entire Church. You're a part of the group.

Father Howard: And only at Mass can you receive Jesus in the Eucharist.

C.J. Carbone: But it's so boring! The songs are so dull. It's always the same.

Pat Carlson: You kids drive me crazy when you say that! You'll spend five hours playing video games, but you can't even give forty-five minutes at Mass once a week? And when you go, you sit in the back, don't sing, don't pay attention, and talk through the whole thing. You're not getting anything out of it because you're not putting anything into it.

Mike Dabrowski: Wait a minute. We're not here to criticize but to try and improve the liturgy. Let's make a list of ways it could be better.

Frank Zura: But we can't just stop there. We should also think about some things each of us could do to get more involved in our parish's celebration of the Mass. We can't wait for somebody else to take care of everything. We're all responsible.

Imagine you are at this meeting. What suggestions would you make to improve your parish's liturgy?

_____

_____

What could you do to get more involved and help make the celebration more meaningful? Check off the actions you would choose.

_____ sit closer to the altar

_____ pay attention to the readings and the homily

_____ join the choir or music group

_____ become a lector

_____ donate money to help support your parish

_____ participate in the songs and responses

_____ receive Communion

_____ other: _____

Follow this discussion by directing everyone's attention to "Why Go to Mass?" on page 16. Ask seven volunteers to role-play the characters in the scene.

After the role-play, elicit responses to the following or similar questions.
- Which person's lines can you most relate to? Whose do you disagree with the most?
- What reasons do these individuals give for going to Mass? What do you think of their responses?
- If you were at this meeting, what would you have said?

Then have the group members answer the two questions at the end of that section. Brainstorm together a list of suggestions for improving their parish's liturgy. The checklist of ways to get more involved in the eucharistic celebration could be completed privately. Without asking group members to reveal their own choices, you could ask the group to comment on each action. You may wish

to communicate the young people's suggestions to parish leadership.

For the closing prayer, have ready a loaf of soft-crusted bread. After gathering the group into a circle, invite one member to read John 6:53–56. Then, starting with yourself, share one of the petitions from page 14. Instruct the group to respond to each petition with "Lord, hear our prayer." After each person's petition, he or she can break off a piece of bread and pass the loaf to the next person. A person may choose not to share aloud by simply breaking the bread and passing it on in silence.

Once the loaf has been shared among the group members, invite everyone to offer one another a sign of peace and friendship. Close by holding hands and praying the Lord's Prayer together.

FOCUS

Catholics express their relationship with God in many ways.

PRAYER, PRESENCE, DEVOTION

Objectives

To help the participants:
- recognize God's presence in our world;
- become familiar with various forms and styles of prayer;
- identify the holy days and seasons of the liturgical year.

Materials Needed

chart paper, markers, audio and/or video recording equipment (for Breaking the Ice) • Bible • art supplies (paper, paints, colored pencils) • pens/pencils paper • a variety of Catholic sacramentals • candle and matches

Session Outline

Breaking the Ice   (15 minutes)
- Create an advertising campaign for the Catholic Church.

1. Starting Out   (10 minutes)
- Read the story of an artist's attempts at "Picturing God."
- Name situations and events that remind us of God's presence ("A Sacramental World").

2. Exploring   (20 minutes)
- Complete a survey on "How to Build a Friendship."
- Focus on ways to maintain a relationship with God in "God Talk."
- Discuss and create examples of the four kinds of prayer.
- Examine various forms of Catholic prayers and devotions ("Prayer Styles").
- Identify the holy days and seasons of the liturgical year ("Church Seasons").

3. Connecting   (15 minutes)
- Use a "wordgram" to review various Catholic beliefs and practices.
- Optional Activity: You may extend the session by adding the Optional Activity.
- Participate in a prayer service that introduces various Catholic sacramentals.

Breaking the Ice

Ask the group members to create an advertising campaign for the Catholic Church. Have them work all together or in small groups to create newspaper, magazine, radio, or television ads highlighting some positive features of the Church and encouraging people to become part of the Catholic faith community. Provide materials—from chart paper and markers to audio and video recording equipment, if possible—to enable the young people to present their ads to the rest of the group members.

Background for Session 5

God Talk

By the very nature of divinity, a definition of God transcends all human understanding. Yet, it is only through our fallible human expressions that we are able to speak about God. As a result, we are faced with questions such as: Is God a he? A she? Neither? Both? Is God a judge? A peacemaker? A lover? Is God omnipotent? If so, why does God allow evil to exist? If not, how can God be God? Issues such as these about the divinity are the stuff of great debate today—as they were yesterday, as they will be tomorrow.

In the classical terms of our Christian faith, we believe that God is triune: three Persons in one God—Father, Son, and Spirit—a God who is our Creator, Redeemer, and Sanctifier. That agreed, our faith invites us to encounter the divine reality in our lives as individual believers and as a community of believers.

Prayer Talk

Prayer is an integral part of encountering the divine. As noted in earlier sessions, the sacraments, with the Eucharist at their center, offer us powerful encounters with God. Yet, the other rituals of the Catholic Church—liturgy of the hours, devotions to Mary and the saints, sacramentals, and so on—witness to a long tradition of formal worship, public and private. Not to be ignored, either, is the Church's tradition of less formal prayer, including meditation and contemplation.

Although they are probably more consciously aware of the Church's ritual prayer, young people are not strangers to informal prayer; they just may not have thought about it in any concrete way. It may help to remind them that encountering God in prayer can be almost limitless in its manner and place. Likewise, prayer can occur in the midst of any human emotion. Whenever we take the time to reflect and assess what's happening in our lives in the context of God's presence with us, we are praying.

Not Just Words

The relationship with God that is nurtured in prayer cannot be selfish. Of course, limited by our humanity, we sometimes may be tempted to fashion a Santa Claus God

with whom we bargain for goods as in a bazaar. Nevertheless, a more mature perspective sees that our encounter with God is two-way. Younger adolescents can begin to grasp this, since they themselves are starting to relate with one another and older people on a more mature and mutual basis.

Likewise, our relationship with God has a purpose that includes our personal needs—but extends beyond those needs. Prayer involves not just words but actions of love as well, and actions must flow out of our prayer experience and reflect our encounter with God, who is love. It is noteworthy that the prayer Jesus taught his followers, the Lord's Prayer, focuses on God <u>and</u> one another, using the first person plural, *us,* rather than the singular *I* or *me.* Younger adolescents are just leaving the natural self-centeredness of childhood, but they may be introduced to this other-centered and active component of prayer.

Reflections

1. How would I describe God to a nonbeliever? How does my image of God affect my prayer experience?
2. What forms of prayer do I use most often? Why am I comfortable with these forms?
3. If I were to tell the young people in my group just one thing about prayer, what would it be? Why?

Picturing God

Sarah, age 13, was walking through Evergreen Park when she spotted an artist painting alongside a tree. Felipe, the artist, noticed her and asked, "How are you today, my young friend?"

She didn't say much. Then she asked Felipe, "Can you paint me a picture of God?" Felipe asked Sarah to return the next day at the same time.

Sarah was anxious for the time to pass. She headed for the park the next day as the artist had asked. On the big easel stood a covered painting. As Felipe greeted her, Sarah said, "I'd like to see God."

Felipe unveiled a painting filled with bright, colorful spring flowers and birds. Sarah looked puzzled and said, "I thought you said you would paint a picture of God." Felipe asked her to return tomorrow.

Sarah left disappointed but did as Felipe asked. The next day, Felipe showed her a painting of children playing hopscotch on the sidewalk in front of a row house.

"Where's God?" Sarah, clearly annoyed, demanded. Felipe told her again to come back tomorrow. Sarah muttered as she left, "He's just a con artist." But she did return. This time he showed her a painting of a family gathered for a meal. "I guess you don't know God," Sarah exclaimed.

A Sacramental World

We encounter God in so many ways: in the beauty of nature, in the joy of children, in the love of family members, friends, and others who care about us. The world is full of events that remind us of God's constant presence. Powerful ocean waves crash along the shore at high tide. A man or woman in a wheelchair enters and finishes the Boston Marathon. A homeless family finds food and refuge in a shelter and their lives begin to turn around. These are some of the moments when we can see and feel the goodness of God's presence in our world.

Can you name a time or place when you felt especially close to God?

Why do you think many people feel God's presence in nature? Do you?

17

---

1 **Starting Out** (10 minutes)

Ask the group members to quietly read the story of Sarah and Felipe in the section, "Picturing God," on page 17 in the YOUTH MAGAZINE.

Review each of Felipe's paintings (the flowers and birds, the children playing, and the family meal) and talk with the young people about what Felipe may have been trying to express about God. What (if anything) do these paintings say to them about God? What pictures would the group members have painted?

Distribute sheets of paper and markers, paints, or colored pencils. Ask each person to use these materials to create a work of art that represents God to him or her in some way. (The group members will be invited to explain their artwork during the closing prayer.)

Next, ask one or two volunteers to read aloud "A Sacramental World." Invite comments on the reading,

asking the members of the group to name other situations or events that could be reminders of God's presence in our world.

Discuss with the young people the two questions at the end of that section. For the first question, invite group members to recount personal stories of feeling especially close to God, but don't force anyone to share.

Alternative: Distribute pens or pencils and sheets of paper and ask the participants to answer the first question in more detail. Volunteers could share their stories anonymously by handing in what they've written. You can then shuffle the papers, select several at random, and read them to the group for their comment.

How to Build a Friendship

It's not enough to simply see and feel God's presence. Each of us is invited to have a personal friendship with God. But close relationships with anyone can be hard work. We need to develop them all the time and never take them for granted. Friends have to communicate, spend time together, and try to understand each other.

Think of a close friend or family member. How do you and this person keep in touch and maintain a relationship? (Check the ones that apply.)

____ We talk a lot on the telephone.
____ We spend time doing things together.
____ We confide in each other.
____ We help each other when one of us is in trouble.
____ We stick up for one another.
____ We lend each other things without worrying if they'll be returned.
____ We share our feelings.

God Talk

Our relationship with God is also very special. God is closer to us than any friend. We can communicate and keep in touch with God through prayer. When we pray, we show our love by talking with God. We say these things to God:

"I think you're great!"

"I'm sorry I'm not always a good friend."

"Thanks for everything."

"Help!"

We can pray alone or with others, day or night, in church or anywhere else, in times of crisis or times of peace. We can use Scripture or memorized prayers (such as the Lord's Prayer and the Hail Mary) or we can simply talk to God spontaneously in our own words. We can silently listen to God, too.

When do you talk to God? What do you talk about?

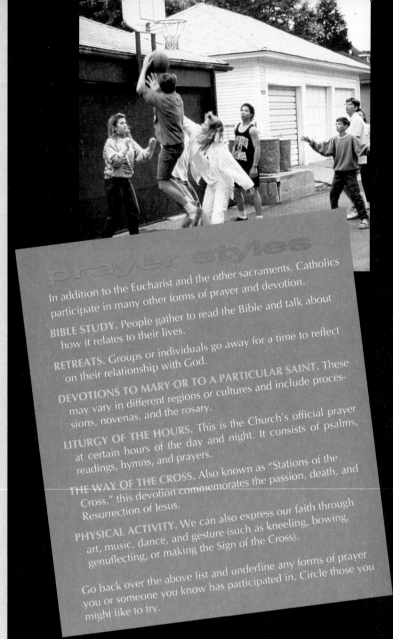

prayer styles

In addition to the Eucharist and the other sacraments, Catholics participate in many other forms of prayer and devotion.

BIBLE STUDY. People gather to read the Bible and talk about how it relates to their lives.

RETREATS. Groups or individuals go away for a time to reflect on their relationship with God.

DEVOTIONS TO MARY OR TO A PARTICULAR SAINT. These may vary in different regions or cultures and include processions, novenas, and the rosary.

LITURGY OF THE HOURS. This is the Church's official prayer at certain hours of the day and night. It consists of psalms, readings, hymns, and prayers.

THE WAY OF THE CROSS. Also known as "Stations of the Cross," this devotion commemorates the passion, death, and Resurrection of Jesus.

PHYSICAL ACTIVITY. We can also express our faith through art, music, dance, and gesture (such as kneeling, bowing, genuflecting, or making the Sign of the Cross).

Go back over the above list and underline any forms of prayer you or someone you know has participated in. Circle those you might like to try.

---

2 Exploring (20 minutes)

Ask the group members to read quietly "How to Build a Friendship," on page 18, and complete the survey. Tally the results with a show of hands. Connect this material on maintaining a relationship with the next section, "God Talk," which focuses on our relationship with God.

Begin a discussion on prayer by directing everyone's attention to the four kinds of prayer (praise, contrition, thanksgiving, and petition) illustrated in that section. Ask the group members to think about when, why, and how they pray. Invite volunteers to share their thoughts with the others. (Note that some young people consider this a very personal topic, so don't force anyone to share. Also, you may find that talking about "a relationship with Jesus" rather than "a relationship with God" might work better with some members of your group.)

Divide the participants into four smaller groups and assign one kind of prayer to each group. Have the members of each group work together to write a prayer in their assigned category. Each group should select a representative who will read their prayer at the end of the session.

The section "Prayer Styles" on page 18 describes various forms of Catholic prayers and devotions, which may be more or less familiar to the group members. Review these prayer styles with the participants, adding to the list any other forms of prayer the group members can name. (You may wish to concentrate on those devotions that are practiced in your parish.) If the young people seem interested, you could help them plan and participate in one or more of these prayer activities, possibly in association with other parish groups.

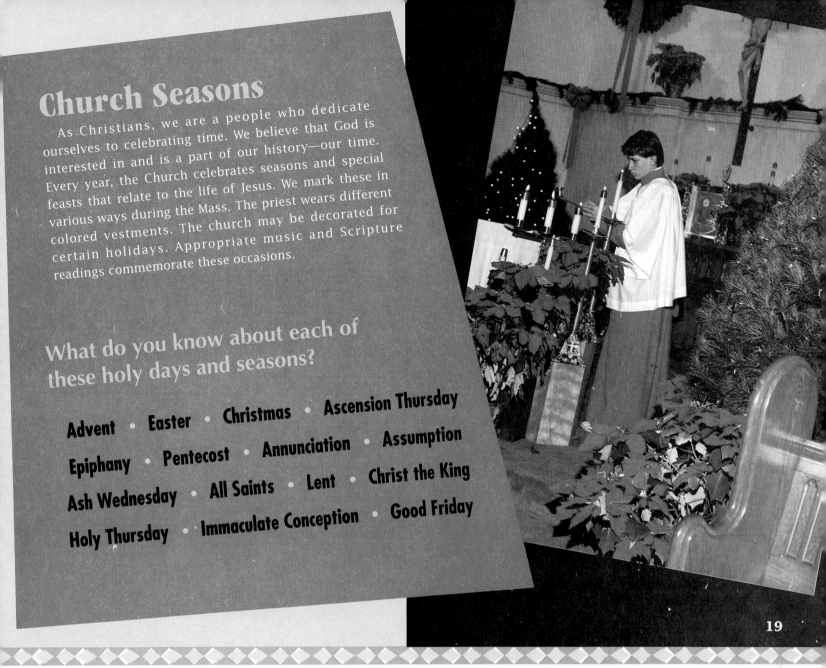

Church Seasons

As Christians, we are a people who dedicate ourselves to celebrating time. We believe that God is interested in and is a part of our history—our time. Every year, the Church celebrates seasons and special feasts that relate to the life of Jesus. We mark these in various ways during the Mass. The priest wears different colored vestments. The church may be decorated for certain holidays. Appropriate music and Scripture readings commemorate these occasions.

What do you know about each of these holy days and seasons?

Advent • Easter • Christmas • Ascension Thursday
Epiphany • Pentecost • Annunciation • Assumption
Ash Wednesday • All Saints • Lent • Christ the King
Holy Thursday • Immaculate Conception • Good Friday

Ask the group members to look over the section "Church Seasons" on page 19 and tell you what they know about each of the holy days and seasons listed. Depending on the time of year, you may wish to focus on current or upcoming celebrations.

Alternative: The group members could form two teams and play a game similar to *Jeopardy* about holy days and liturgical seasons. One team could write a definition for one of these words, and the other team could try to name the correct holy day or season.

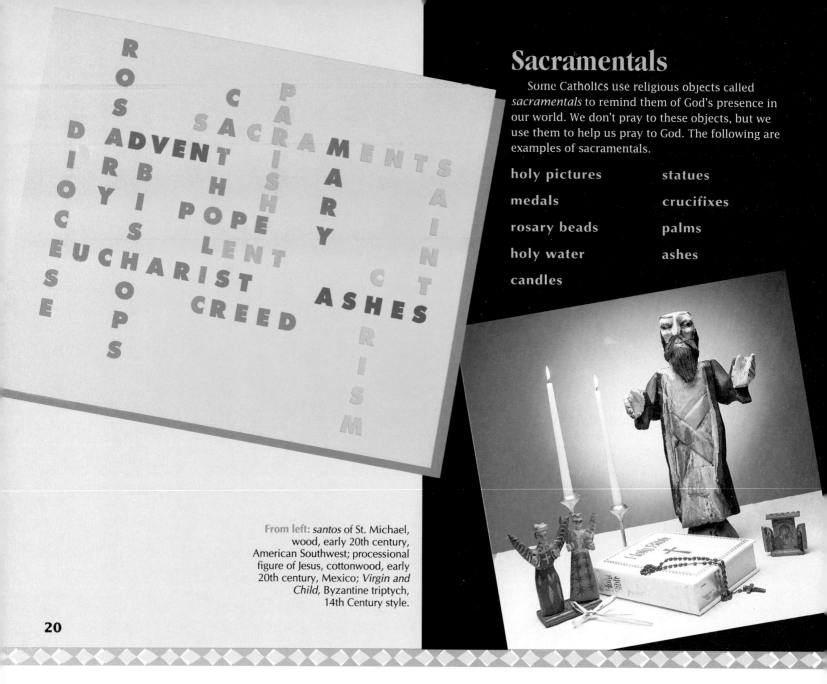

The wordgram contains the following words:

ROSARY
DIOCESE
ADVENT
DERBY
ARCHBISHOP
SACRAMENTS
PARISH
POPE
LENT
EUCHARIST
CREED
MARY
ASHES
SAINT
CHRISM

Sacramentals

Some Catholics use religious objects called *sacramentals* to remind them of God's presence in our world. We don't pray to these objects, but we use them to help us pray to God. The following are examples of sacramentals.

holy pictures	statues
medals	crucifixes
rosary beads	palms
holy water	ashes
candles	

From left: *santos* of St. Michael, wood, early 20th century, American Southwest; processional figure of Jesus, cottonwood, early 20th century, Mexico; *Virgin and Child*, Byzantine triptych, 14th Century style.

20

3 Connecting (15 minutes)

The "wordgram" on page 20 can provide the group members with an opportunity to review various aspects of Catholic belief and practice. Divide the participants into two teams, one for the horizontal words and one for the vertical words. Each team must correctly define or explain each of their words. You may want to set a time limit, give prizes to the team that finishes first, or provide reference materials. Group members could create their own wordgrams.

Direct everyone's attention to "Sacramentals." Talk about the meaning and purpose of the sacramentals listed in that section, as well as any other sacramentals the group members may be familiar with. (Some of the participants might be wearing religious jewelry.) Remind them that sacramentals don't have "magical" powers, but can help us pray to God.

Optional Activity *You may extend the session by adding the following activity.*

Arrange for your group to tour the church or other parish buildings, identifying and discussing the sacramentals they find along the way.

For the closing prayer, gather everyone into a circle around a table displaying several sacramentals as well as the artwork that the group members created at the beginning of the session. You may wish to dim the lights, light a candle, and play some quiet, reflective music. Allow the young people to examine each of the sacramentals; then invite several volunteers to explain their artwork. After some time for silent prayer and reflection, ask the four representatives to each read the prayer that was written by his or her group earlier in the session.

FOCUS

We can't just say we're Catholics; we have to live our faith.

OUT OF THE PEWS

Objectives

To help the participants:
- see that living our faith is a lifelong journey;
- know the corporal and spiritual works of mercy;
- appreciate how they can serve others.

Materials Needed

chart paper and markers (for Breaking the Ice) • Bible • paper and pens/pencils • brochures of local social service agencies (for the Optional Activity) • a bowl of water

Session Outline

Breaking the Ice   (15 minutes)
- Imagine creating a theme park called "Catholicland."

1. Starting Out   (10 minutes)
- Discuss ways to tell what someone believes in by the way he or she lives ("Only on Sunday?").
- Read "Doing Good Works" and review the corporal and spiritual works of mercy.
- Evaluate ways group members could put their "Faith into Action."

2. Exploring   (20 minutes)
- Learn about Catholic relief efforts in "Building Compassion."
- Brainstorm a list of "Problems, Problems, Problems," in the local community, as well as potential solutions.
- Read the story of Anthony Day in "Getting Involved."
- Optional Activity: You may extend the session by adding the Optional Activity.

3. Connecting   (15 minutes)
- Review some key aspects of what it means to live as a Roman Catholic Christian.
- Think about ways to put faith into action in "Make a Difference!"
- Reflect on the question, " What does it mean to be a Catholic?"
- Read " . . . And We Are the Church" and participate in a blessing ceremony.

Breaking the Ice

Invite the young people, working all together or in smaller groups, to imagine creating a theme park called "Catholicland." This theme park could be divided into sections (such as "The World of the New Testament," "Twenty-first Century Church," "Church History Land," and "Sacrament City"). The group members could describe each section of the park, suggesting features such as rides, attractions, costumes, souvenirs, and so on. You could tape a number of sheets of chart paper together upon which the group members could illustrate their ideas for "Catholicland."

A Focus on Others

In its Pastoral Constitution on the Church in the Modern World, the Second Vatican Council declared: "While helping the world and receiving many benefits from it, the Church has a single intention: that God's kingdom may come, and that salvation of the whole human race may come to pass" (*Gaudium et Spes*, #45). This affirmation directs us toward the communality that is inherent in the Church's life and mission. But as the bishops of the Council plainly note, the Church is not focused on the community of believers alone, but on the community of all humanity.

The Christian community's mission of service to others is rooted in Jesus' own mission while extending back to the social teachings of Judaism as expressed by the Law and the Prophets. The Gospels are replete with examples of how Jesus concretely showed concern and sought justice for others. He valued the needs of people—needs which lie at the heart of the Mosaic Law—even above the legalistic requirements of any rule or regulation. Knowing that some people were discriminated against, he consciously reached out to the alienated, bringing to them the love of God.

Contemporary Undertakings

As people who profess to follow Jesus, we are compelled by the Gospels to be just toward all people. As a community, the Church—universal and local—has sought to do this, albeit imperfectly, throughout its history. For instance, the Campaign for Human Development, which includes an annual voluntary collection in parishes, has distributed millions of dollars to groups all over the country as seed money to start programs and help people. Likewise, the Catholic bishops in the United States have in recent history debated and published pastoral letters on nuclear arms, the economy, and racism, which have stirred people's thinking both inside and outside the Church.

These are just some of the thousands of initiatives that have resulted from the Second Vatican Council and the Church community's grappling with the good news in light of today's world. At the heart of all the charitable works that have been the hallmark of the Church and renewal in the Church is the Council's call to make God's kingdom become more real and effective in our world.

A Personal Mission

All these global issues, while stimulating and challenging, might be elusive for the average Catholic and especially for a young person. The world around us isn't philosophical or theoretical. It's very real. We often see homeless sleeping in alleyways or on doorsteps. Elderly people sit by themselves in malls or parks. Poor children play without supervision or direction.

Even these realities of life in the United States may be too abstract for younger adolescents to grasp. They may well be aware only of things closer to home: a friend who is made fun of because he or she is different; a parent who is unemployed or trying to raise a family alone; a sibling who is addicted to drugs. These situations call us to ask, "How often do I take those close to me for granted or fail to treat them as Jesus would?"

Our response as Christians should be grounded in the Gospel. We are called to proclaim "good news" to those in despair, to those who are apathetic or indifferent. We may live in a global world, but our reality is very local—as local as our home and neighborhood.

Reflections

1. For me, what is the most poignant Gospel story that shows Jesus promoting justice?
2. How would I rate the Church's record on social justice? My own record?
3. What are some concrete things young people in my group can do to grow in their insight into the Church's social mission?

Only on Sunday?

Going to church. Reading the Bible. Praying. Celebrating the sacraments. All of these are ways we express our Catholic faith. But what does it mean to live as a Catholic every day, in our homes, among our friends, in our schools and neighborhoods? These are the places where our faith is put into action. Here is where Jesus comes alive through each one of us.

Jesus himself brought religion to the people. He wanted everyone to know that how we live is more important than what we preach. Jesus gave us the ideal to live by: "Love one another as I have loved you" (based on John 13:34).

Being a Catholic doesn't just mean praying or going to Church. We show that we're Catholic Christians every day, in everything we do. As Catholics, we're challenged to do something to make a difference. We're called to make our faith come alive in the everyday events of our lives. How can we do this?

- **in the way we live, act, and treat others every day**
- **with what we decide to do with our time, talents, and money**
- **through our choice of a career, lifestyle, or vocation**

21

1. Starting Out (10 minutes)

Begin the session by asking the group members, "Could anyone tell, by observing the way you live, that you're a Catholic? If so, how? Do you think that people should be able to tell what someone believes in by the way he or she lives?" Encourage them to give examples to support their opinions. After this discussion, ask everyone to read quietly "Only on Sunday?" on page 21 of the YOUTH MAGAZINE. Go over any questions or comments that may have been sparked by their reading.

Point out to the group that, as Catholics, we are called to make our faith come alive in our daily lives. Direct everyone's attention to the bulleted list at the end of that section. Divide the participants into three smaller groups. Have each group suggest some specific, concrete ways we can live our Catholic faith in one of the three situations described in the list. (Each group could act out a scene based on one of their suggestions.)

Alternative: Divide the participants into pairs or small groups and ask them to write, then act out, a dialogue between a Catholic and a non-Catholic on the topic, "What does it mean to be a Catholic?"

Doing Good Works

In our everyday lives, we can respond to people's needs by practicing the corporal and spiritual works of mercy. These are ways we can care for one another's bodies, minds, hearts, and spirits.

The Corporal Works Of Mercy

- Feed the hungry.
- Give drink to the thirsty.
- Clothe those who lack clothing
- Help those in prison.
- Shelter the homeless.
- Care for the sick.
- Bury the dead.

The Spiritual Works of Mercy

- Help sinners.
- Teach those who need to learn.
- Give advice to those who need it.
- Comfort those who suffer.
- Be patient with others.
- Forgive those who hurt you.
- Pray for the living and the dead.

Faith Into Action

Place a **+** next to the actions you've already tried, a **?** next to the ones you might consider, and a **–** next to the ones that are probably not for you.

___ Pray every day.

___ Shop for a neighbor.

___ Attend Mass each week.

___ Read the Bible.

___ Forgive people who hurt you.

___ Share your possessions with others.

___ Learn about the Church.

___ Make a donation to charity.

___ Help at a local food pantry.

___ Baby-sit children during Sunday Mass.

What are other ways you could put your faith into action?

_____

_____

_____

_____

Building Compassion

Throughout its history, the Catholic Church has tried to meet peoples' needs. Hospitals and schools were built. Missionaries were sent to faraway lands. Refugees were welcomed. Many individual Catholics, rich and poor, contributed to support these efforts. All of these services are still being provided by the Church today. Some are done throughout the world and some are done on the local level.

Local churches try to help the people in their neighborhoods. Some set up food pantries or soup kitchens. Parishioners volunteer to visit the elderly and homebound, running errands and doing chores for them. Clothing drives collect clothes for thrift shops and shelters, especially during winter months.

Take another look at these last two paragraphs. Which of the works of mercy can you find? Which are happening in your parish or community?

Problems, Problems, Problems

Every generation faces many problems and concerns. In the United States, one of the richest countries on earth, many children and their families go to bed hungry. People suffer discrimination because of their skin color, age, gender, religion, or nationality. Workers lose jobs. Families break up. Drugs, gangs, and violence destroy communities. Homeless people beg and live on the streets. Natural resources are wasted. Land, water, and air are polluted. We contribute to some of these problems. But we also can contribute to the solutions.

22

Next, ask a volunteer to read aloud "Doing Good Works" on page 22. Review the corporal and spiritual works of mercy and ask the group members to name some ways that people their age could practice these works. You could also have the young people refer to the parable of the sheep and the goats (Matthew 25:31–40), from which the list of the corporal works of mercy is derived.

Alternatives: The group could try a Scripture search to find examples of Jesus and the disciples practicing these works of mercy, or they could look for contemporary examples in current newspapers and magazines.

Ask everyone to read "Faith into Action" and complete the exercise. (You could also ask them to name the work of mercy each item represents.) Talk about the group members' current involvements and the actions they might be willing to try in the near future.

2 **Exploring** (20 minutes)

Ask one or two volunteers to read aloud "Building Compassion." Help the group to focus on local needs and services by discussing the following questions.
- Which of these works are now being carried out in your parish or community?
- Which should be done to help meet local needs?
- Which might be necessary in the future?

Divide the participants into smaller groups of three or four persons. Ask each group to brainstorm a list of the challenges their community faces. (The section "Problems, Problems, Problems" could provide some ideas.) Tally the responses to arrive at a list of the most pressing local problems. Give the group members an opportunity to say what they think should be done about these problems (they may wish to express their opinions to local leaders). Be sure to also mention what is already being done.

Getting Involved

Anthony Day has visited Mexico three times. None of these trips were vacations. The first time, he helped paint Santa Juanita's Church in Nueva Rosita, a coal-mining town of 60,000 people in the northern part of the country. On his second trip, Anthony helped to arrange for six Mexican teenagers to spend a summer vacation in his family's home near the New Jersey shore. During his last visit to Mexico, he helped dig the foundation for an addition to the church.

Anthony Day's service began when a college professor invited him to volunteer in a soup kitchen in his home town. "My eyes were opened to the real world," Anthony told a group of friends. Anthony describes his life and faith as average. He enjoys school but doesn't get too involved. He goes to church on Sundays. But he noticed that his faith became more real once he got involved in helping others.

"It's my duty as a Christian," says Anthony. "You get to understand what all the Scriptures mean when you're helping others."

How did Anthony's actions increase his faith? Can you see yourself getting involved in a similar way? If you can, how? How might this affect your faith?

TOP: Day, third from left, with other volunteers and parishioners, in front of the church they painted.

MIDDLE: Anthony Day, left, takes a break from helping to build an addition to Santa Juanita's Church.

LEFT: Anthony Day, center, surrounded by a Mexican family and a coworker.

Give the members of the group some time to quietly read "Getting Involved" on page 23. When everyone is finished reading, discuss the questions at the end of that section.

Alternative: Invite a guest speaker from the parish or local community who has worked on a similar service project to talk about his or her experiences.

Optional Activity *You may extend the session by adding the following activity.*

Obtain brochures from several different local social service agencies. Distribute these to the members of the group and discuss the work these organizations perform. You may also be able to arrange for a guest speaker from or a visit to one of these agencies.

MAKE A DIFFERENCE!

Living out one's Baptism as a Roman Catholic Christian takes a lifetime. It involves some key ingredients.

- believing that Jesus is our savior
- celebrating his presence in our lives and in our worship
- living as part of the Christian community founded in Jesus' name
- loving and serving others as Jesus did

Our religion means little unless we live it. Catholic Christians live their faith by helping others and building community. It all comes down to each person living his or her faith in the world. Personal commitment makes a difference. And we don't have to go to Mexico or to the inner city to get involved. We're not expected to do everything. But, as Christians, we <u>are</u> expected to do <u>something</u>. There are many things we can do that will make a difference in the lives of others. Here are just a few.

- **Spend a few hours a week visiting sick people in a hospital or nursing home.**
- **Start and staff a nursery on Sunday mornings to baby-sit children while their parents attend Mass.**
- **Join together to maintain a neighborhood park by picking up litter and keeping the area clean.**
- **Be friendly to classmates who seem lonely or who are ignored by others.**
- **Organize a toy, food, or clothing drive at school or in your church.**

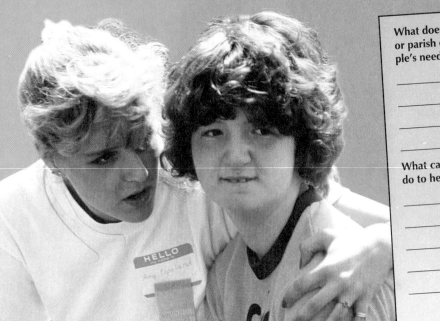

What does your family, school, or parish do to help meet people's needs?

_____

_____

_____

_____

What can you and your friends do to help?

_____

_____

_____

_____

_____

_____

_____

...And We Are the Church

FOR A WORLD at its worst, we need a Church at its best...

FOR A WORLD full of sadness, we need a Church full of gladness...

FOR A WORLD that complains, we need a Church that cares...

FOR A WORLD full of war, we need a Church that's full of peace...

FOR A WORLD full of heartache, we need a Church that's full of hope...

FOR A WORLD full of "bad news," we need a Church that's full of "good news...

FOR A DISCOURAGED WORLD, we need an encouraged Church...

BISHOP J. TERRY STEIB OF MEMPHIS,
CHAIRMAN OF THE
U.S. BISHOPS' COMMITTEE
ON BLACK CATHOLICS

---

3 **Connecting** (15 minutes)

The first paragraph of "Make a Difference!" on page 24 mentions some key aspects of what it means to live as a Roman Catholic Christian. Review briefly with the group members some of the things they've learned in these sessions about being a Catholic.

The remainder of that section suggests some ways that young people can put their faith into action. Together, answer the two questions at the end of that section. (This is a good opportunity to get the group involved in planning and carrying out some sort of parish service project.)

Gather the group into a circle for prayer. Distribute sheets of paper and pens or pencils. Provide some quiet reflection time for each person to answer the question posed by the title of this theme, *What Does It Mean to Be a Catholic?* When everyone is finished writing, invite volunteers to share their responses.

Bless each group member by dipping your fingers into the bowl of water and tracing the sign of the cross on his or her forehead. (Or, the group members could bless one another.)

Ask one person to read " . . . And We Are the Church" on page 24, with the rest of the group responding after each verse, "And we are the Church."

Close by sharing a sign of peace and friendship.

> To help us serve you better, please evaluate this theme by completing and mailing the postage-paid questionnaire that appears on the last two pages of this GUIDE.

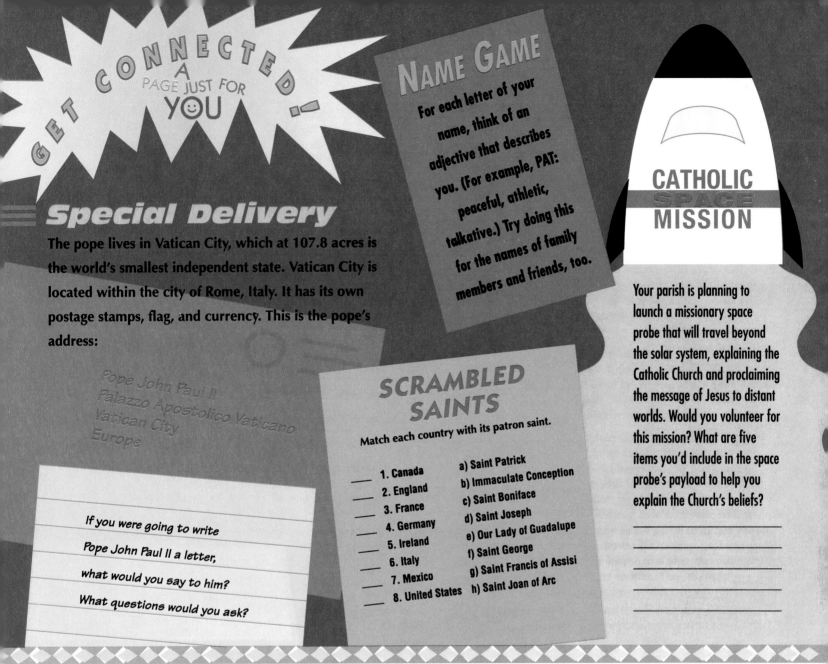

GET CONNECTED!
A PAGE JUST FOR YOU 😊

Special Delivery

The pope lives in Vatican City, which at 107.8 acres is the world's smallest independent state. Vatican City is located within the city of Rome, Italy. It has its own postage stamps, flag, and currency. This is the pope's address:

Pope John Paul II
Palazzo Apostolico Vaticano
Vatican City
Europe

If you were going to write Pope John Paul II a letter, what would you say to him? What questions would you ask?

NAME GAME

For each letter of your name, think of an adjective that describes you. (For example, PAT: peaceful, athletic, talkative.) Try doing this for the names of family members and friends, too.

SCRAMBLED SAINTS

Match each country with its patron saint.

____ 1. Canada
____ 2. England
____ 3. France
____ 4. Germany
____ 5. Ireland
____ 6. Italy
____ 7. Mexico
____ 8. United States

a) Saint Patrick
b) Immaculate Conception
c) Saint Boniface
d) Saint Joseph
e) Our Lady of Guadalupe
f) Saint George
g) Saint Francis of Assisi
h) Saint Joan of Arc

CATHOLIC SPACE MISSION

Your parish is planning to launch a missionary space probe that will travel beyond the solar system, explaining the Catholic Church and proclaiming the message of Jesus to distant worlds. Would you volunteer for this mission? What are five items you'd include in the space probe's payload to help you explain the Church's beliefs?

_____
_____
_____
_____
_____

Scrambled Saints
1. d; 2. f; 3. h; 4. c; 5. a; 6. g; 7. e; 8. b

PROJECTS

Projects in *CONNECT Junior High*

A small-group model of catechesis might have as its philosophy the proverb: "Tell me, I forget. Show me, I remember. Involve me, I understand." One way to extend catechesis beyond the six sessions of a *CONNECT Junior High* theme is to involve the group members in one or more projects related to the theme. These activities provide an opportunity to put into practice the faith content of the theme, helping the group members apply in an active, concrete way the religious concepts they've reflected on and discussed during the sessions.

Some of the benefits of involving junior high adolescents in catechetical projects and activities include the following.

Interaction Working and celebrating as a community can help the young people learn cooperation, build social skills, and observe other Catholics living out their faith. Several of the suggested projects provide intergenerational opportunities within a parish by involving parents and other adults, senior citizens, older teens, and children.

Empowerment Giving the group members a role in planning and organizing the projects can nurture leadership skills. When the young people are each given some responsibility for a portion of an activity, they have a chance to make decisions for themselves and use their own initiative and motivation. Striving toward visible, attainable goals can enhance each person's sense of accomplishment.

Self-Esteem Involving the participants in a number of projects provides the flexibility to accommodate each young person's own learning style and stage of development. Each group member has a chance to discover and use his or her own unique talents and gifts for the benefit of others.

A list of suggested projects related to the topics discussed in *What Does It Mean To Be A Catholic?* follows. You (in conjunction with the members of your group) may choose to use one or more of these projects or to develop an activity of your own. With any project, be sure to prepare the group members adequately beforehand by providing any training, instruction, or explanations they might need. Afterward, allow them opportunities to reflect on and discuss their reactions to the experience. This will help the young people assimilate what they've learned and integrate it into their personal system of belief.

Projects for *What Does It Mean to Be a Catholic?*

- Attend the celebration of one or more of the sacraments. Study and discuss the ritual beforehand; meet afterwards to share observations.

- Designate one Sunday *"CONNECT Junior High Sunday."* Group members can help plan the liturgy, select and lead the songs, decorate the church, and act as lectors, altar servers, and ministers of hospitality. This should not be a Mass only for young people, but one for the entire parish, prepared and led by group members.

- Learn more about the parish by touring the church, rectory, and other parish facilities; attending a meeting of the parish council or other organization; and talking to parish leaders and longtime parishioners.

- Research and write a contemporary meditation on the Stations of the Cross. Group members could present their version of the Stations to the parish during Lent and perhaps videotape or create a slide presentation of their performance.

- Visit an R.C.I.A. group to talk to the catechumens about why they want to become part of the Catholic Church. The group members could ask the question, "What does it mean to be a Catholic?"

- Select an area of Catholic belief or practice to research in more detail. Use the results of this research to write an article or series in the parish bulletin or to teach a religious education class of younger children.

- Plan and lead a prayer service on reconciliation. If possible, provide the group members with an opportunity to celebrate the sacrament of Reconciliation. This prayer service could be celebrated in conjunction with a guest visit by a priest to Session 3 to discuss the sacrament.

- Plan a full or half-day retreat on the theme, "What Does It Mean to Be a Catholic?" If possible, bring the group members away from their usual environment. Provide time for sharing, quiet prayer and reflection, and community-building activities. Close with a Mass or prayer service. (You could involve older adolescents in leading this retreat.)

Notes

Notes

CONNECT Junior High   Catechist's Questionnaire

Please help us continue to develop quality catechetical materials by responding to this questionnaire. Simply remove the questionnaire from the book, fold and tape it as indicated on the reverse, and drop it in the mail. No postage is required.

Thank you for your time and interest.

1. What is the title of the theme being evaluated? _____

2. In what diocese is your parish located? _____

3. What is your parish /community environment? **(Please circle one.)**

    urban   suburban   rural

4. What position do you hold in the parish? _____

5. What is the average number of participants in your group? _____

6. In what grade(s) are the participants in your group? _____

7. How often does your group meet and how long is each meeting? _____

8. To what extent do you use the following? **(Please fill in the letter of the response that best expresses your experience.)**

    (A) ALWAYS   (O) OFTEN   (S) SELDOM   (N) NEVER   (NA) NOT APPLICABLE

    ____ Youth Magazine   ____ Program Director's Manual

    ____ Catechist's Guide   ____ Service Manual

9. How do the participants find the material in the Youth Magazine? **(Circle one.)**   too difficult   just right   too easy

10. The following items refer to the Youth Magazine and Catechist's Guide.   **(Please fill in the letter of the response that best expresses your reaction.)**

    (E) EXCELLENT   (VG) VERY GOOD   (G) GOOD   (F) FAIR   (P) POOR   (NA) NOT APPLICABLE

    ____ Youth Magazine (overall)   ____ Catechist's Guide (overall)   ____ audiovisual resources

    ____ design appeal   ____ organization   ____ session organizers

    ____ appropriateness of photos   ____ introductory material   ____ session backgrounds

    ____ catechetical content   ____ theme overview   ____ session lesson plans

    ____ questions and activities   ____ Get Connected!   ____ theme projects

Note: There is space for additional comments and suggestions on the reverse side.

Additional Comments

FOLD HERE

FOLD HERE

FIRST CLASS
PERMIT NO.197
MORRISTOWN, NJ

POSTAGE WILL BE PAID BY

Silver Burdett Ginn
Religious Education Editor
250 James Street
Morristown, New Jersey 07960-1918

CUT ALONG THIS LINE